D0914990

AMERICAN INDIAN
TOOLS AND ORNAMENTS

AMERICAN INDIAN TOOLS AND ORNAMENTS

*How to Make
Implements and Jewelry
with Bone and Shell*

Evelyn Wolfson

Drawings and diagrams by Nancy Poydar

David McKay Company, Inc.
New York

Library of Congress Cataloging in Publication Data

Wolfson, Evelyn.
    American Indian tools and ornaments.

    Bibliography: p.
    Includes index.
    SUMMARY: Provides instructions for making tools
and jewelry from bones and shells in the tradition
of the American Indians.
    1. Indian craft—Juvenile literature. 2. Jewelry
making—Juvenile literature. 3. Tools—Juvenile
literature. 4. Bone carving—Juvenile literature.
5. Shellcraft—Juvenile literature. [1. Indian craft.
2. Handicraft] I. Poydar, Nancy. II. Title.
TT22.W63   745.55   80-7966
ISBN 0-679-20509-8

Book design: Stacey Alexander

1 2 3 4 5 6 7 8 9 10

Manufactured in the United States of America

To my very supportive family
Bill, Jason, and Dacia

Thanks to Dr. Jeffrey Brain, Curator, Peabody Museum, Harvard University, and Sarah Chalkley Hubbell, Archeologist, for reading and critiquing; to Mike Bilger, Biologist, State Division of Water Pollution Contol, and Dr. Samuel Fuller, Philadelphia Academy of Sciences, for assistance with locating and identifying freshwater mussels; to Lillian and Julian Harwood for assistance with locating marine shells; to Nancy Lewis and Larry Nilson for their bone collections; to Lloyd Jones of Harrison, Idaho, for elk and deer antler; to Sprague Bros., Boston, for steer bones; to Betty McLaughlin for beaver incisors; to Helga and Kristen Volkema and Sean and Deirdre Dundon for working the materials; to Edie Creter for typing; and to Bennett Simon for his perpetual assistance and encouragement.

CONTENTS

INTRODUCTION

While shellfish wear their skeletons on the *outside*, animals wear theirs on the *inside*. Both animal and shellfish skeletons derive their strength from calcium, one of the earth's most abundant elements. Calcium gives bones and shells almost as much hardness as rocks. It is no wonder Native Americans chose bones and shells for toolmaking.

American Indians made tools out of stone, bone, shell, and antler. Each material was chosen for its unique characteristics and workability—not because the materials were readily available.

Bones were particularly suited for tools requiring a combination of strength and resiliency. Hide-fleshing tools are one example. Great pressure was exerted on a hide to remove flesh and hair, yct carc had to be taken not to pierce the skin. Bone scrapers, fleshers, and knives were strong enough to scrape with force, but resilient enough not to puncture.

Bones were universally preferred as a material for needles and awls by Native American weavers. These tools were strong and smooth and could be sharpened repeatedly.

Although it was very difficult to flake stones into small objects, bones were easily cut and shaped into tiny fishhooks, harpoon barbs, and arrowheads—small-sized implements requiring great strength.

Deer and elk antler were the preferred materials for stone flaking because antler is very strong and even more resilient than bone.

Stone toolmakers went to a quarry and chipped away massive pieces of stone for toolmaking. Bone toolmakers were limited by the size and shape of wild animal bones. The largest bone tool was a hoe, made from the shoulder bone of a buffalo. Tribes of the Plains often tilled their gardens with buffalo bone hoes, and Eastern tribes made hoes from the shoulder bones of deer and elks.

Compared with hunting and wild food gathering, shellfishing did not yield great quantities of food, and shellfish were not an important part of the Indians' diet.

Shellfish were gathered during periods of stress. While Native Americans used discarded shells for containers and tool materials, shell tools seem to appear most often during these periods.

Shells for ornamental and ceremonial use, however, were gathered and traded extensively. They had a long-standing importance among tribes as symbols of wealth and position. Ornamental shells were collected for their colors, shapes, and workability. Small brightly colored, warm-water shells, with very strong enamel, were favored for beads and bangles. The shells were ground off at the top and bottom and strung on long cords.

The bright, iridescent interiors of abalone shells were cut into a wide variety of shapes and sizes. Unlike many other shells, abalone does not fracture laterally when cut, and it is relatively easy to work.

Large marine shells, such as conch and whelk, found in prehistoric archeological sites as far inland as Oklahoma, were not casual discards from a mollusk meal. These shells, intricately incised with designs, were made into ceremonial cups, gorgets, and beads. Conch and whelk are extremely thick shells and are difficult to cut even with sophisticated power tools. It is hard to imagine how prehistoric Indians cut these shells with stone tools.

In the Northeast and Southeast, potters incised designs on pots with sharp pieces of bones and shells and scraped and polished their pots with smooth shell fragments.

Clans of the Cherokee tribe have attempted to revive work in bone, shell, and antler, and Indian artists today sell ornaments made from these materials.

A knowledge of the shells used by Native Americans gives a unique perspective to shell collecting. While it takes a great deal of skill to cut and drill tiny shell beads, many simple tools and ornaments can be created from shells collected along the beach or left over from a seashore dinner. Each shell encountered soon presents a potential use as a tool or an ornament.

Once you have worked bone into a strong, sharp tool or strung a series of bones into a piece of jewelry, each bone from the family dinner table may present a creative challenge.

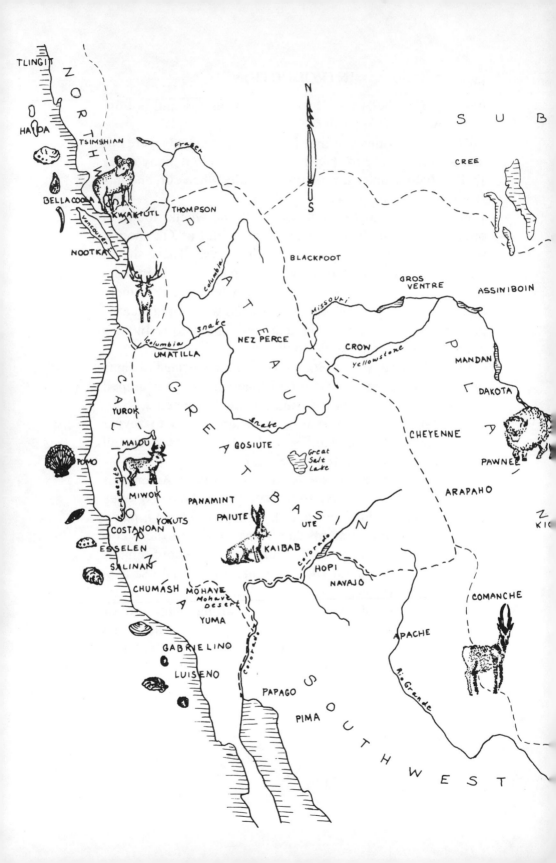

MAJOR TRIBES OF NORTH AMERICA

California-Northwest

Bella Bella
Bella Coola
Chinook
Chumash
Costanoan
Esselen
Gabrielino
Haida
Hupa
Karok
Klamath
Kwakiutl
Luiseño
Maidu
Miwok
Modoc
Mohave
Nootka
Pomo
Quinault
Salish
Salinan
Tlingit
Tsimshian
Wintun
Yokut
Yuma
Yurok

Great Basin-Plateau

Bannock
Cayuse
Flathead
Goshute
Kaibab
Nez Percé
Paiute
Panamint
Shoshone

Shuswap
Thompson
Umatilla
Ute
Washo
Yakima

Southwest

Acoma
Apache
Havasupai
Hopi
Jemez
Jicarilla
Maricopa
Navajo
Papago
Pima
Pueblo
Walapai
Zuñi

Plains

Arapaho
Arikara
Assiniboin
Blackfoot
Cheyenne
Comanche
Crow
Dakota
Gros Ventre
Iowa
Kansa
Kiowa

Mandan
Missouri
Osage
Oto
Pawnee
Quapaw
Santee
Sioux
Wichita
Yanktonnai

Southeast

Apalachee
Atakapa
Caddo
Catawba
Cherokee
Chickasaw
Chitimacha
Choctaw
Creek
Natchez
Pensacola
Powhatan
Seminole
Timucua
Tamathli
Tuscarora
Yuchi

Northeast

Abnaki
Algonkian
Beothuk
Cayuga

Chippewa
Delaware
Erie
Fox
Huron
Illinois
Iroquois
Kickapoo
Malecite
Massachusetts
Menomini
Miami
Micmac
Mohawk
Mohican
Montauk
Narragansett
Neutral
Ojibwa
Oneida
Onondaga
Ottawa
Passamaquoddy
Pennacook
Penobscot
Peoria
Pequot
Piankashaw
Potawatomi
Prairie
Sauk
Shawnee
Seneca
Susquchanna
Wampanoag
Winnebago

Bringing in a whale in Neah Bay, Washington. (Smithsonian Institution)

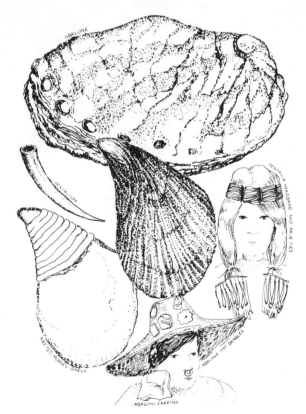

Shells of the northwest coast and their uses.

1

NORTHWEST

Tribes of the Northwest Coast built fishing villages on sheltered bays and islets along the rugged Pacific coast, from northern California to Yakutat Bay, Alaska. Food was obtained by fishing and whale hunting; travel was done by wooden canoe. In the spring and fall, salmon, cod, halibut, herring, smelt, and olachen spawned in freshwater rivers and streams throughout the region.

Spawning fish, especially salmon, were often followed by gams, or herds, of killer whales. These animals, really large dolphin, can be distinguished by a dorsal fin that is lacking in true whales. Tribes of the area knew when killer whales were offshore because their prey—seals and white whales—retreated to shore. The killer whale was an important figure in Haida folklore, appearing on wooden boxes and totem poles. Only the giant sperm whale and bull walrus were unafraid of the killer whale.

From November to March, gams of sperm whales pass the shore of Vancouver Island, bound for summer in the Arctic. The Nootka, Makah, and Quinault tribes of Vancouver Island were famous for hunting whales in sturdy wooden canoes. Whalers, covered with large bearskin robes, threw long harpoons with antler-barbed points into the whales. The barbed points became detached and the harpoon shaft fell away. Some tribes hunted whales in the one hundred-mile-long Juan de Fuca straits between Vancouver Island and the northwest coast of Washington. Other tribes collected carcasses washed ashore.

Northwest Coast tribes also hunted sea lions and seals that spent the winter on rocky islets or in protected fjords. Unlike whales, sea lions and seals must return to land or a block of ice to bear their young. Sea lions spend the daylight hours resting and preening on the rocks; at night they feed on fish, especially squid.

Whalebone and the bones of other sea mammals were important to tribes of the Northwest. Beaver incisors and finely chipped stone were set into whalebone handles, then wrapped with spruce root. Cedar bark was beaten with whalebone shredders to make it soft enough for weaving.

Rich mud flats, where rivers meet the sea, produced quantities of clams and mussels. In Puget Sound, tribes gathered ten-inch mussels in dense clusters in the shallow waters. Mussels were eaten raw, roasted, or smoked. They were also dried on cedar strings and stored away for winter. Mussel shells were cleaned and used as dishes, ladles, and spoons. Mussel and clamshells were also sharpened on sandstone to make knives and arrowheads. Cedar or spruce root was wrapped around the shell hinge to form a grip. Nootka tribes fitted spears and harpoons with sharpened shells, and broken fragments were often used for adzes, chisels, and scrapers. Tribes of Vancouver Island used shell knives to carve curious little wooden images placed over graves.

Scallops that live in deep water were not collected along the Coast, but their shells were often picked up onshore. Coastal tribes traded the shells with inland tribes, who used them for rattles that kept bears away from fishing traps.

Ornaments of shell were highly prized throughout the region. Local abalone, small and pale compared to California abalone, was used for inlays in wooden boxes and bowls. The eyes, teeth, and nostrils on wooden masks were also inlaid with abalone. When traders brought California abalone to the northwest coast in the nineteenth century, tribes of the region started to make large pendants, earrings, and nose rings from the flat iridescent centers of the shells.

Dentalia, or tusk shells, are usually found in deep waters, but they were collected at several locations on the seaward side of Vancouver Island at moderate depths. The unusual occurrence of dentalia in the area may be due to special ocean currents. The Nootka used special tools to gather the tiny, fragile animals. Because the hollow little shells were so rare, they were in great demand as trade items. Six-foot strands of dentalia were used for money. The tip of the shells were ground off, then strung on cords. Or the shells were cut into small, bead-like pieces and suspended from the ears or from a hole in the nose. Dentalia ornaments were an indication of great wealth among tribes of the northwest coast.

The dense cedar forests of the region provided tribes with readily available, easy-to-work material for homes, canoes, and household utensils. Woodworking tools were very important and highly specialized along the coast. A site on the Fraser River in British Columbia yielded jadeite, a serviceable stone for toolmaking. Tribes that did not have access

Elk.

Elk bone and antler uses.

to workable stone, either traded for it or substituted bone, antler, and shell. Along the coast, deer and elk were driven down mountain trails to valleys where they were killed. This saved packing the heavy carcasses down the mountain. In Puget Sound, even women and children hunted deer and elk from canoes, when the animals tried to swim from the mainland to Vancouver Island.

Antler is made into awls and wedges.

Inland tribes had greater dependence on hunting than fishing and often traded surplus animal material to coastal tribes for fish and shellfish. Deer and elk bones were used for fishhook barbs, projectile points, needles, pendants, awls, and rings. Cannon bone, the strongest bone of deer and elks, was used for harpoons and arrowheads.

Wealthy members of the Salish tribe wore woven wool blankets around their shoulders and fastened the blankets with curved bone or antler pins. The natural curve of antlers gave it extra strength when several layers of material had to be held together.

Antlers were often gathered in the forests from February to April, when the animals shed their massive horns. Antler is easy to cut, shape, and carve when taken from freshly killed animals. Antlers increase in size each year. A mature stag often carries a heavy set of six-tined antlers, each four feet in length. Because the part of the antler closest to the animal's head has the greatest strength, it was used for wedges to cut long, straight-grained wooden planks. Smaller antler wedges, made from the tine, or tip of the antler, were used to split small planks and to hollow out bowls, masks, and canoes. Antlers made perfect tool handles because their naturally rough exterior provided a good gripping surface. The soft inner core of antlers was hollowed out and a piece of stone or beaver incisor inserted in

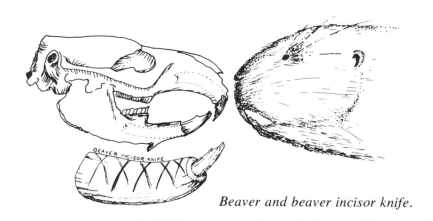

Beaver and beaver incisor knife.

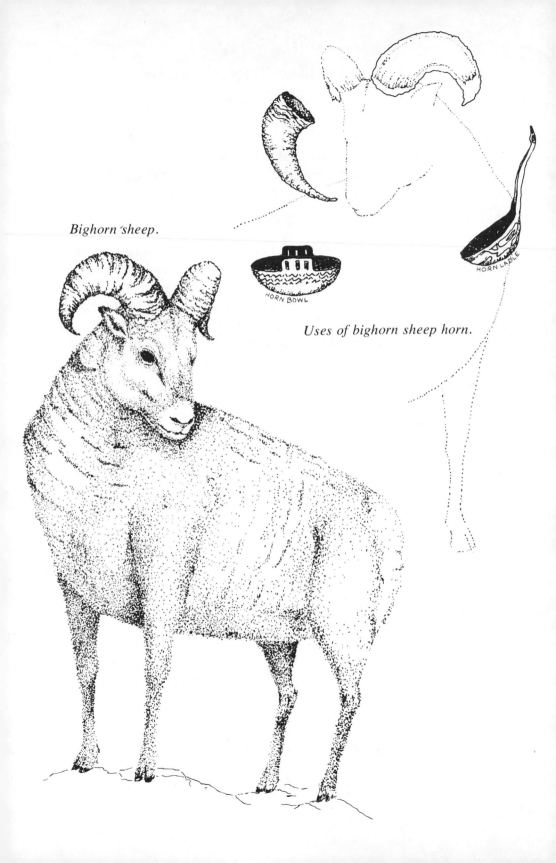

Bighorn sheep.

Uses of bighorn sheep horn.

HORN BOWL

HORN LADLE

the center. Spruce gum was used to set the blade in the handle, which was tied with cedar or spruce root cordage.

Beavers, muskrats, and porcupines have strong, chisel-like teeth to cut wood, and the tribes of the region used the teeth for the same purpose. The upper teeth, which have too much curvature, were discarded, but the lower incisors were inserted in wood and antler handles and used for carving.

Bearskins were valuable because they were large enough to cover the whole body without being sewed. Bearskin was also a favorite material for ceremonial costumes. Bear claws, teeth and bones were made into necklaces by wealthy and important tribal members.

Along the northern coast, sheer rock cliffs formed the backdrop for Tlingit and Tsimshian villages. These tribes hunted bighorn sheep in high mountain meadows. Rough, concave hooves give the bighorn good traction for browsing on steep slopes. Unlike deer and elks, which have solid, spiked antlers that are shed each year, the bighorn has massive spiral horns. The bony core of sheep horn, attached to the head, is covered with a rough outer sheath. This shiny, black sheath was prized as a material for bowls, ladles, and spoons. When the hollow sheath is softened in hot water, it can be molded and shaped.

Adornments of bones, antlers, claws, and teeth were important indicators of wealth throughout the region. Men and women wore gracefully carved antler pendants around their necks or attached to their clothing. Rings and beads were cut from bird bones. Bone and antler combs were popular hair ornaments. Wealthy women wore labrets—round, cylindrically-grooved pieces of bone or wood—in a slit in their lower lip. Small labrets were replaced with successively larger ones until elderly women of rank wore three-inch-long labrets with comfort. Shamans, or medicine men, carried whale bone, bear teeth, and antler charms to help them communicate with supernatural beings.

8

2

CALIFORNIA

The tribes of California enjoyed fishing, shellfish gathering, and hunting sea mammals along the many miles of warm-water coast. These abundant coastal resources, as well as inland animals, seeds, berries, and other wild plants, allowed tribes of the region to gather food in a leisurely fashion all year round.

Wood and serviceable stone and large quantities of good plant and shrub material for weaving were readily available throughout the terrain. Basket-weaving was the primary industry of California; weavers of the area were among the most skilled artisans in North America. Finely-woven baskets were used for cooking, storing and gathering food, and for ceremonial purposes. Awls, made from deer and elk bones, were the California Indians' most important tools.

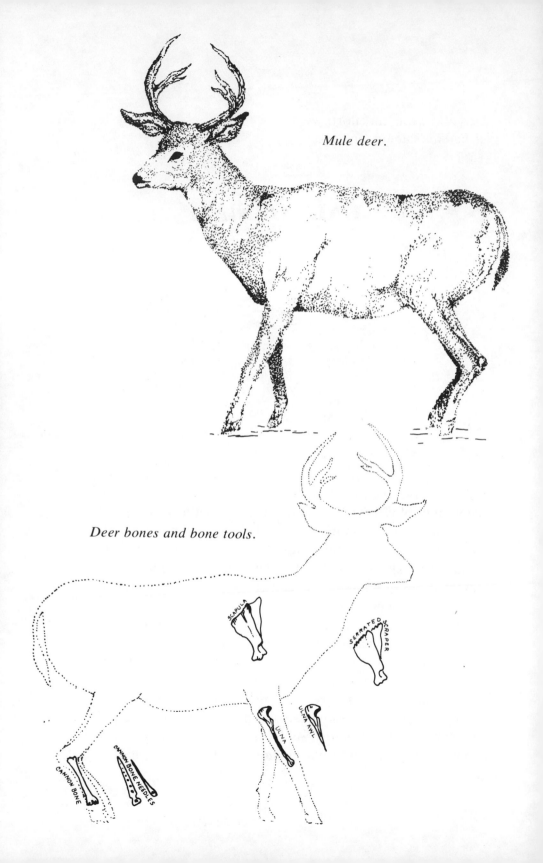

Mule deer.

Deer bones and bone tools.

CALIFORNIA

Tribes of northern California closely resembled their neighbors on the northwest coast, who worked wood, fished for salmon, and accumulated ornaments that symbolized wealth and position.

King and chinook salmon, caught with bone or antler harpoons and a variety of woven nets, were plentiful along the Smith, Klamath, and Eel rivers. The tribes living along these rivers had woodworking kits that included stone axes, bell-shaped stone mauls, and elk wedges. Karok woodworkers split wooden planks with antler and carved wooden boxes, paddles, and spoons with stone and horn knives. They also made spoons out of various materials: wood, elk kneecaps, elk antlers, deer skulls, and sometimes mussel shells.

Yurok tribes, living near the mouth of the Klamath River, traded seaweed (for its salt content), surf fish, and shellfish with inland Hupa tribes. Occasionally, dentalia from Vancouver Island were used in trade. Each dentalium was valued according to its length; lengths of less than one inch were too small for currency. The Hupa, in turn, supplied the Yurok and other coastal tribes with acorns and vegetal foods. Large shell middens, or heaps, south of Point Conception in Monterey Bay, attest to the importance shellfish played in the diet of north coastal tribes. Sea mammal bones, found in the shell middens, suggest that whales were hunted along the shore.

A long narrow valley, surrounded by mountains, dominates the northern three-quarters of California. Tribes of the region gathered seven different species of acorns and hunted the year round. In winter and spring, deer and elks fed along valley fringes. They were stalked by solitary hunters, who used bows and stone or bone-tipped arrows. Snares and brush fences were also popular devices for catching these large animals. Roosevelt elk occupied the north coast from California to Vancouver Island, and tule,

11

or dwarf elk, lived in the marshlands of the Sacramento and San Joaquin valleys. There, herds of pronghorn antelope grazed on the rich grasses.

There were few large animals in southern California because sparse rainfall limited plant growth and attracted only small rodents. Coast live oak and Englemann oak were the only trees in the southern ranges, but their acorns were the least preferred by any tribe. The Chumash and Gabrielino, who lived along the southern coast, from Santa Barbara to San Diego, enjoyed shorefish, shellfish, and sea mammals. Sea otters and seals were common on off-shore islands. Quantities of abalone, Pismo clams, oysters, scallops and California clams were gathered from the warm southern waters.

The Chumash tribes of the San Miguel, Santa Rosa, and Santa Cruz islands (off the coast of Santa Barbara) navigated heavy seas between the islands and the mainland in sturdy ocean-going canoes. Abalone shells, valued raw material for many tribes, were particularly abundant on the islands. The large valves of Pismo clams, abalones, and California clams were used as containers. The natural holes in the side of an abalone shell, where the animal excretes water and body waste, was plugged with asphaltum—a cement used by many North American tribes. Asphaltum appears in scattered globs or pools, where it seeps through bedrock as a result of natural geological processes. The largest pool in California is the La Brea Tar Pits in Los Angeles, from which the remains of mastodons, saber-toothed tigers, woolly mammoths and other species of Pleistocene life erupted.

Many everyday items, including tool handles, were elaborately inlaid with abalone. Scrapers, made from the outer edge of abalone shells, were worn around the neck. The natural curve of the shell was ground smooth on native sandstone. A hole was then drilled in one end, and the

Maidu girl, wearing an abalone shell necklace and head-band. Her belt is also decorated with abalone shells. (Smithsonian Institution)

Abalone pendants.

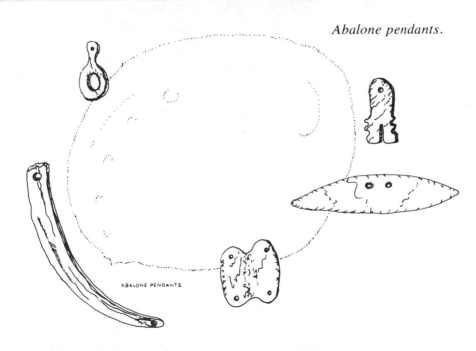

ABALONE PENDANTS

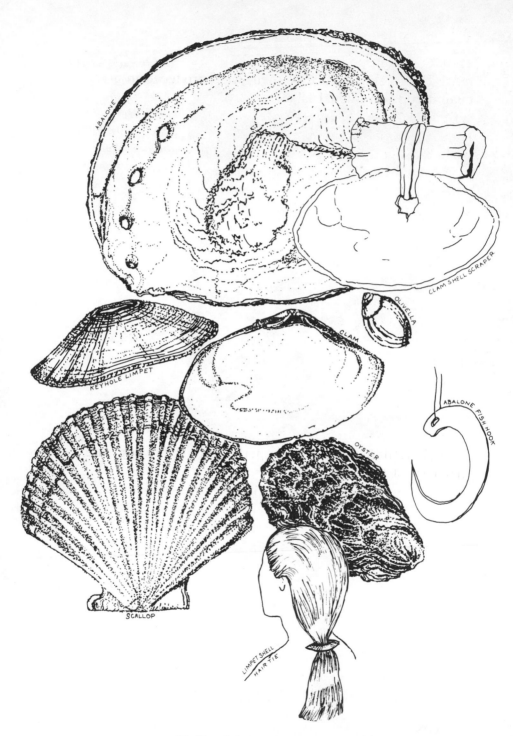

Shells of California and their uses.

scraper was suspended from a cord. Abalone fishhooks, made from a single piece of shell, were produced in great quantity on San Miguel Island.

Coastal Chumash tribes used bone-headed harpoons and fishhook barbs to catch bonitos, yellowtail, sharks, and barracuda in the Santa Barbara Channel. Forty-five-foot pilot whales migrated into the Channel in winter, but were too dangerous to pursue in the rough waters. Sea lions and seals were killed on the islands with large, whalebone clubs.

Shell beads, important to tribes throughout North America, were made for thousands of years before the arrival of European explorers. Brightly colored shellfish inhabit warm waters, and southern California tribes collected many of these beautiful species. Olivella, a tiny, brightly colored univalve found in shallow, muddy water, were abundant in southern California. The hard shells of the olivella contain large quantities of enamel, which makes it very difficult to work. Only one bead was made from each shell, the top and bottom being ground off to form the bead. Chumash tribes sewed the tiny shell beads onto bags.

Keyhole limpets, naturally perforated at the top, are members of the snail family. Water is drawn into the bottom side of the shell and passed out through the natural opening at the top. Keyhole limpets were made into hair ornaments by grinding out the size of the center hole.

Shell disc beads were cut from clam and mussel shells and were used as currency by several California tribes. Thin, cylindrical clam shell beads, up to 3¼ inches long, were sometimes worn by men and women in a pierced nose hole. These beads were very difficult to make and extremely valuable.

Along the coast, tribes of the Chumash hunted deer and birds. Their bones were used to make fishhooks, scrapers, and pins. The scapula, or shoulder bone, of the deer was

This Pomo artisan uses a pump drill to perforate shell beads.
(Smithsonian Institution)

notched along one edge to form a saw. Because the Chumash were proficient basket weavers, they also produced quantities of fine deer and bird bone awls. The natural notch on the proximal end of a deer ulna bone, or the end closest to the animal's heart, is grooved where it attaches to the humerus. This notch made a perfect finger grip. The eyes of bone sewing needles were cleverly counter-sunk to prevent the weaving thread from wearing.

Bone knives, scrapers, needles, and awls.

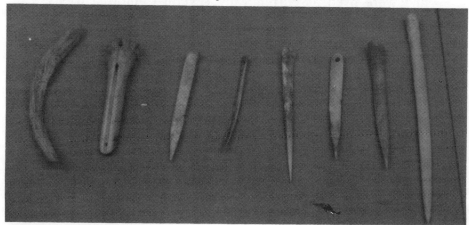

3

GREAT BASIN-PLATEAU

Plants are small and shrublike in the Great Basin, where few large animals live. The region is cold and dry in winter and hot and dry in summer. Plants and animals, adapted to the rigors of the region, are especially skilled at surviving without water for long periods. The limited resources of the Great Basin created a restricted life-style for the area's nomadic tribes.

Grass, shrubs, and animal bones were readily available materials, and a few tribes had access to workable stone and wood. Basket-weaving probably developed as a natural response to the need for lightweight containers.

Indians of the Great Basin used their weaving skills to create household utensils, clothing, and nets for snaring

17

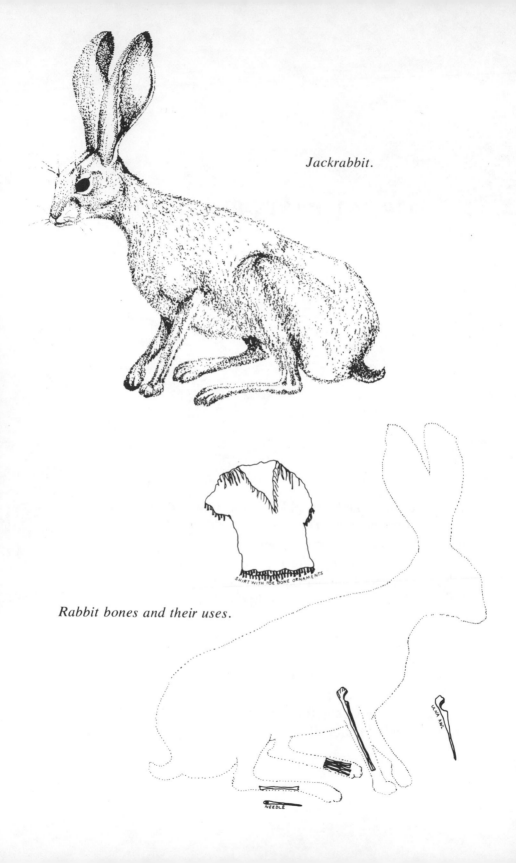

Jackrabbit.

Rabbit bones and their uses.

SHIRT WITH TOE BONE ORNAMENTS

ULNA AWL

NEEDLE

small animals. Rabbits were important sources of meat, fur, and bones. Jackrabbits are particularly well-suited for desert life because they rarely need water. They can survive in areas where there is limited vegetation because they are able to run fast, without obstruction, and escape their predators. Jackrabbits feed on the greasewood, rabbit brush, mesquite, and sagebrush found throughout the region. Nets, woven of plant fibers, were strung across stakes, and the rabbits were driven into the nets. Rabbit bone awls and needles were the most important tools of the weaver.

The Goshute, who lived along the southwestern edge of Great Salt Lake, had few plant or animal resources, but they had serviceable stones that they worked into knives and drills. Stone was flaked in the palm of the hand (protected with a piece of hide) with an antler tool. The stone tools did not have handles. Instead, they were wrapped in animal skin where they were gripped.

The Goshute seized every possible opportunity to hunt deer and elk. If antelope and mountain sheep occasionally wandered into the region, their bones, antlers, and horns were used to make tools and ornaments. Fleshing tools were fashioned out of the cannon bones of deer and elks; awls were made from bone splinters and antlers. The Goshute also made ladles from the shoulder blades of deer or elks.

Southern Paiute tribes, who lived at the foot of the Kaibab plateau, hunted mule deer with bows and arrows. Hunters attracted the deer by blowing on a leaf to imitate the cry of a fawn. After the animals were killed, they were skinned and dressed before they were carried home. The flesh was piled inside the hide and the legs were tied together.

Northern Paiute tribes, living along the Snake and John Day rivers, had greater food sources because they caught spawning salmon. But these tribes never developed a

Bone salmon spear.

method for preserving the salmon. They continued their seasonal migrations for food by moving into the mountains when the salmon season was over.

Great Basin tribes may have traded their baskets for shells because they were in possession of shell beads and ornaments for thousands of years. Very old archeological sites in Utah have yielded quantities of olivella and abalone beads and pendants, shell material that comes from the California coast. In addition, whole and worked freshwater mussel shells were found in Utah sites.

California desert tribes, living along the Arizona, Utah, and Nevada borders, attached bone, shell, and stone dangles to clothing. The dangles jingled when the wearer walked or danced. Walapai women obtained dentalia and olivella shells for dangles from the Mohave Indians. Unworked, olivella shells were strung into necklaces—favorite pieces of jewelry among the women. When shell was not available, Paiute, Shoshone, and Walapai women created dangles out of deer and rabbit toe bones and dew claws.

20

The bones were hardened in hot ashes. Walapai women made special dancing belts with bear claws that jangled, and they edged their dresses with wildcat bones. When the Europeans arrived, dangles made of natural materials were replaced by small metal bells or pieces of scrap metal.

It is believed that some of the shell discs found in the Great Basin were worked in California and traded to Basin tribes. Pine nuts, fruit pits, and seeds were often used in combination with shells and bones. The Shoshone made beads out of bones, shells, animal claws, and fish vertebrae. Some tribes pierced the earlobes of infants and inserted soft thongs strung with shell, bone, and animal claws. Walapai warriors pierced their nasal septum, and wore a single bead or shell in the hole to make them look fierce. They also tied back their hair with strands of shell, bone, or stone beads. Southern Paiute tribes wore bead bracelets of bone, shell, and stone.

On the Columbia Plateau north of the Great Basin, tribes were less nomadic because there were more food sources. Fish spawned in the whitewater rivers and streams, that cut deep canyons and in the plateau's canyons were deer, elk, bears and beavers, as well as a variety of plants and shrubs. Annual food-gathering activities in the plateau region required less year-round travel than in the Great Basin.

Bones and antlers were used to make tools and ornaments. Edible camas roots were dug with antler root diggers. Bird and deer-bone awls were important tools for Nez Percé weavers, who created soft, flexible bags out of Indian hemp.

Black bears were hunted in the forests and uplands of the Bitterroot and Seven Devils mountains and along major waterways. In winter, when food supplies were particularly low, some hunters were brave enough to crawl into the den of a sleeping bear and kill it.

Beavers were plentiful along mountain streams all year

Above Left:
Don Lelooska Smith be-
gins work on a mountain
goat horn spoon.

Above right:
Don Lelooska Smith
carves a horn spoon after
it has been molded.

Left:
Don Lelooska Smith's fin-
ished spoon.
(U.S. Department of the
Interior, Indian Arts and
Crafts Board)

around. They were valued for their fur, meat, and tough little teeth, used for making knives by Indian carvers.

Tribes of southern Washington hunted mountain goats in the Cascade Mountains. The shiny black outer sheaths of

Nez Percé shell necklace. (Eastern Washington State Historical Society)

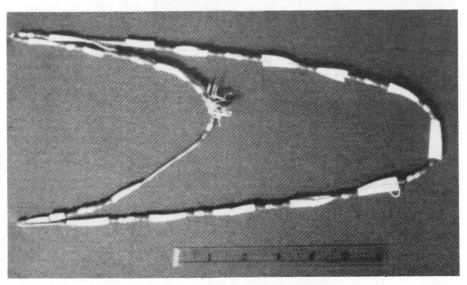

Nez Percé dentalium-and-bead necklace. (Eastern Washington State Historical Society)

Pio Pio Tolekt, of the Nez Percé tribe, wearing a dentalium necklace and breastplate. (Idaho Historical Society)

the slightly curved horns were molded and carved into beautiful spoons and scoops.

Spring and summer were the major buffalo-hunting seasons of the Nez Percé and other tribes of the region. Supplies of buffalo meat and hides were brought back to the Plateau region and traded with tribes of the lower Columbia River.

The Nez Percé traded animal hides for quantities of dentalia shells and abalone from the Pacific Coast. Tribal leaders wore necklaces and breastplates made of dentalia and traded beads. Abalone and other shells were made into pendants, necklaces, and earrings.

24

4

SOUTHWEST

About the time of Christ, Hohokam farmers built elaborate irrigation ditches along the Salt, Gila, Santa Cruz, and San Pedro rivers in Arizona, where they raised two crops of corn each year. In the northern region, their neighbors, the Anasazi, planted small gardens in a region cut by deep canyons and high mesas. A third group of desert farmers, the Mogollon, farmed the rugged foothills of the Mogollon Mountains that swing south and east into southern New Mexico.

Many forms of animal life flourished in the Southwest: Merriam's elk, buffalo, antelope, bighorn sheep, Mexican Mountain sheep. Native deer, mule deer, grizzly bears, and black bears were common in the mountains. Wild turkeys

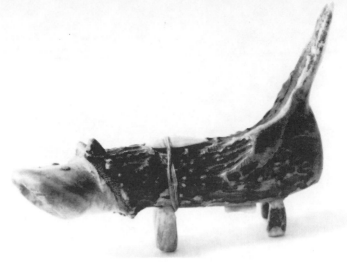

Deer antler fetish in the form of a reptile, with turquoise inlays for eyes and a stone arrowhead attached to the back. It was worn by a Zuni hunter to give him success in the chase. (U.S. Department of the Interior, Indian Arts and Crafts Board)

Bone beads.

Bone awls and their uses.

Splitting bone to make tools.

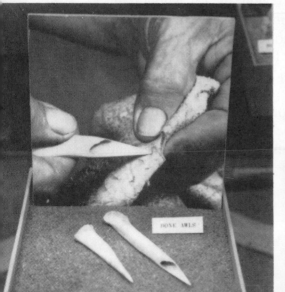

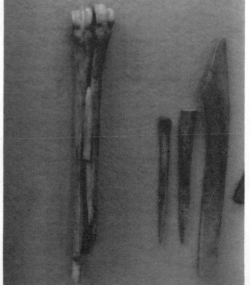

were also plentiful, and prairie chickens abounded in the eastern plains. Waterfowl fed and rested in ponds, lakes, and streams along traditional migration routes. While many of these animals still inhabit the Southwest, some are extinct.

Desert farmers supplemented their corn crops by hunting and gathering wild food. Men went on seasonal hunting expeditions, while young boys hunted and trapped small animals close to home. Among the Zuñi, it was customary to paint one bone from the first animal killed by a young warrior.

Wood and serviceable stone for tool making were scarce in the Southwest. Therefore, animal bones, horns, antlers, and shells were important raw materials. Many large mammal bones, used as hammers and clubs, were left in their natural state; smaller 'bones and antlers were worked into tools and ornaments. Deer, antelope, and bison ribs were sharpened along one edge on native sandstone and used as cutting knives. Awls, needles, and chisels were made from split bone, the concave-convex structure of split bones giving them great strength. Bone scoops were made from the femur of wildcats or lynxes by removing the balls at the joint ends of the bones and working down the other ends. The butt of an antler, where it breaks away from the animal's head, was used as a polishing device. Awls were also made from the fibulae of wildcats and the ulnae of coyotes. Very elaborate awls, with handles, were made by inserting a turkey bone into the joint end of a large deer bone. Bone battans, used to separate warp threads when weaving, were made from cylindrical sections of mammal bones. The battans were often engraved with geometric or circular grooves.

Indians of the Southwest also created beautifully carved and polished bone ornaments. Rings, intricately carved or painted, were made from the pelvic bone of rabbits, or cut

ABALONE

Shells of the Southwest
and their uses.

OLIVELLA

CONUS

PENDANT

OLIVELLA AND ABALONE NECKLACE

BRACELET

BRACELET

PENDANT

GLYCERMERIS

Reaming.

from large animal bones. Small bird bones were made into beads by scoring a length of bone, then cutting and polishing it. Bone pendants were fashioned from wildcat and antelope skull. Flat, square pieces of bone, probably the scapula of deer or elk, were perforated at two corners and suspended around the neck. These pendants were polished on both sides and incised with designs. Stone tools were used to grind and cut the bone, and holes were drilled in it with cacti spine. After the introduction of iron by the Spanish, bones and antlers were only used for tool handles.

The giant sea that once filled the desert of the Southwest left behind thousands of fossilized shells that still remain scattered throughout the region. While some of these shells were used as ornaments by prehistoric tribes, most shell material was obtained through trade or by traveling to the Gulf of California and to the California Coast. The Hohokam became the chief traders in shell material and the most skilled artisans of shell jewelry. They also collected Glycymeris, a variety of olivella shells, and abalone from the Gulf of California. Olivella and Conus shells, very beautiful in their natural state, were often left unworked. Sometimes the tip of the shell was ground away and the shells strung on long cords.

A shellworker's tool kit included a variety of stone implements. Sandstone and schist, common rocks in the Southwest, were natural abrading materials, used to file, drill, grind, and ream. Reamers, rounded pieces of sandstone tapered at one end, were used to grind away the center of a shell leaving a thin rim.

Many exquisitely carved and polished bracelets have been uncovered in archeological excavations throughout the Southwest. The surface of a glycymeris valve was first incised with a sharp file, then the shell was tapped away. Or the face of the shell was rubbed on a sandstone slab, creating a large hole in the center. The hole was enlarged with a

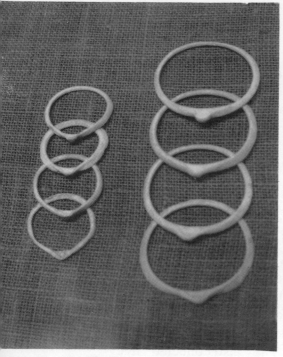

Shell bracelets.

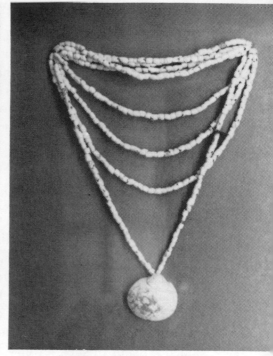

Shell necklace.

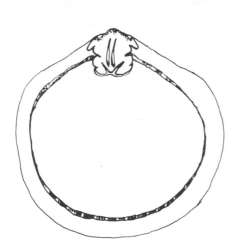

Shell bracelet and glycymeris shell.

reamer, worked in a circular motion. The umbo, or hinge region, was usually carved with figures of water birds, frogs, and snakes. Stone, antler, and hardwood were used as hammers, chisels, and knives. Quartz was often used for engraving. Small holes were drilled with a cactus spine or the point of a yucca leaf. These natural drills were later replaced by the bow drill. Abalone-shell pendants were made by cutting the shells into discs, ovals, triangles, and rectangles, then holes were drilled.

The Anasazi obtained most of their shells through trade with the Mogollon, who, in turn, got them from the Hohokam. The Anasazi favored the small, brightly colored olivella shells from the Gulf of California. Anasazi artisans worked two hard stones, turquoise and jet, because these materials were more readily available. Turquoise deposits in northwestern and southwestern Arizona provided them with ample quantities of material for beads and pendants. Jet, a shiny black stone, was obtained from surface coal deposits. Jet, turquoise, and shell were all worked in the same manner.

The Mogollon, who worked many of the same kinds of shells used by the Hohokams, also made jewelry with turquoise and jet. They obtained some of their turquoise from the Anasazi sites in Arizona and from two areas in north-central and southwestern New Mexico.

Beads are probably the most difficult item to fashion out of shell or stone because they crack, even though they are very hard. Beads made from olivella shells were scored with a sharp stone into tiny squares. Sometimes the beads were drilled into small squares before the shell was broken; at other times, the shell was snapped off, then drilled. Drilling beads before they were made into squares was risky, since the shell did not always break cleanly. The tiny squares were strung tightly on a cord and rubbed back and forth on a sandstone slab until they were round and smooth.

A Zuni man uses a pump drill to perforate turquoise. (Smithsonian)

This process took a great deal of time, patience, and skill.

Today, the Indians of Santa Domingo and Jemez Pueblo north of Albuquerque, continue to make stone and shell beads in the traditional way. Some have also adopted the use of power tools. Power tools, however, require a great deal of skill because shell heats up very fast and can easily crack with high-speed tools. The shells are cut into squares with a hacksaw; holes are drilled with an electric drill on a drill press; and the string of beads are carefully placed against an electric sanding wheel. Each of these steps requires a good deal of knowledge about shell material, as well as expertise with power tools.

5

THE PLAINS

Early white settlers were unprepared for the miles of dry, grassy prairie west of the Mississippi River, where travel was measured in months rather than in miles. From Mexico to Saskatchewan and from the foothills of the Rocky Mountains to the Mississippi Valley, there were 1,250,000 square miles of flat grasslands. Eastern prairie grass was so high that a man on horseback had to stand in his stirrups to see over it. Tall grasses diminished in size in central Kansas and along the western borders of the Dakotas. Only short, hardy grass grew on the flat western Plains in the shadow of the Rocky Mountains.

For fast-moving, grass-eating animals, the Plains were a natural habitat because prairie grass withstands heavy graz-

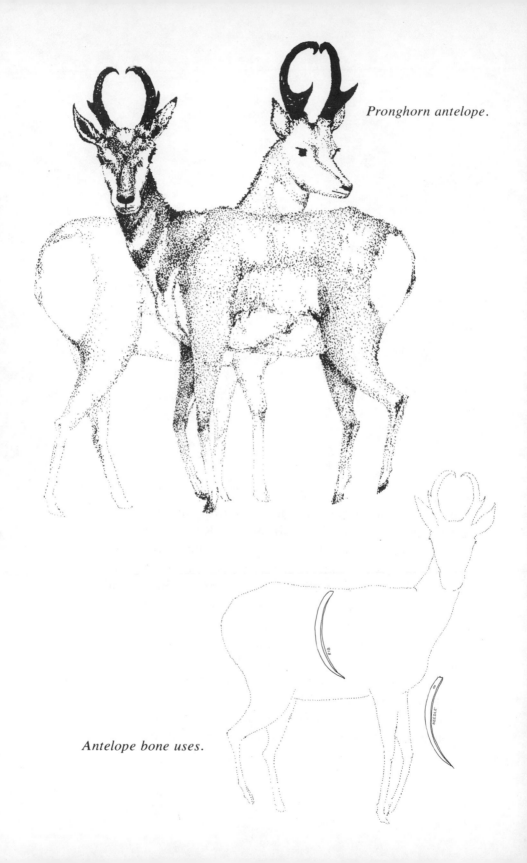

Pronghorn antelope.

Antelope bone uses.

ing; roots grow deep underground and new tissue growth remains just below the surface. Prairie dogs, pocked mice, kangaroo rats, and ground squirrels burrowed under the land; well-camouflaged birds, grasshoppers, and insects hid in the thick grass to escape their predators: the grizzly bear, kit fox, badger, black-footed ferret, snake, coyote, owl, and hawk. Antelope, buffalo, and deer fed on the rich grass, outrunning their enemies, wolves and coyotes.

Unlike any other animal in the world, the antelope sheds black outer sheaths from its horns annually. The antelope's hollow sheaths are pushed away each year from the base to make way for new growth. Permanent, bony cores, covered with a soft, thick membrane, harden into new horns. As the animal matures, the horn sheaths become heavier and longer.

Lightning fires once routinely burned over large areas of the Plains, stimulating new growth, rich in nutrients. Tribes in the region observed the buffalo's preference for grazing in burned-over areas and adopted the practice. Annual burning kept seedling trees and shrubs from infringing on the Plains in the north and along the eastern borders. Only tribes of the western Plains restricted burning because the semi-arid grasses of the area were too fragile.

For thousands of years, Native Americans of the Plains pursued buffalo, the largest land mammal in the New World, over the rich grasslands. The buffaloes travel in large herds, mate in the summer, and bear one offspring at a time in the spring. Males often weigh 2,200 pounds, and females sometimes weigh as much as 1,100 pounds. Both male and female buffaloes have hollow horns; the female's horn is more slender and curved than the male's. Buffalo-horn tools were used by tribes of the Blackfoot to flatten decorative quills freshly attached to hides.

Before the acquisition of the horse, only a few tribes penetrated the heartland of the Plains. Most Indians maintained

Buffalo.

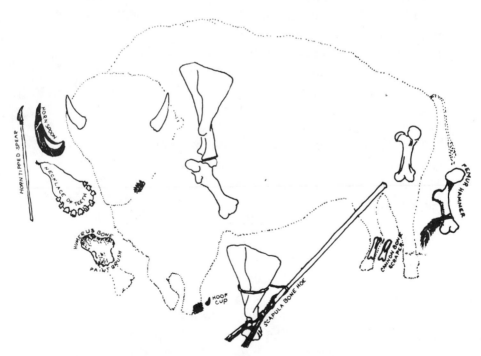

Tools and ornaments made of buffalo bone, horn, hoof, and teeth.

Blackfoot horse travois. (Smithsonian Institution)

permanent farming villages and hunted on foot. Dogs were used as burden animals, and a small wheel-less cart, called a travois, was attached to the animal's shoulders to carry supplies. Traveling with dogs was difficult, however, because they tended to chase after small animals.

The Cheyenne and Crow of the southern Plains were the tribes first to acquire runaway Spanish horses in the mid-sixteenth century. Horses were perfectly suited for Plains life because they, too, flourished in the rich grasslands. In addition, horses had more endurance than buffaloes and could run faster. They could also be easily trained to carry hunters and heavy supplies.

Buffalo eventually became the focus of all material and spiritual life on the Plains. The Cheyenne, Crow, Arapaho,

Assiniboin, Blackfoot, Comanche, Gros Ventre, Kiowa, Sarsi, and Teton Sioux abandoned farming and adopted completely nomadic life-styles. Tribes in the northwestern plateau region, the Kutenai and Flathead, traveled into the western grasslands to hunt. Tribes on the eastern fringes of the Plains—the Arikara, Hidatsa, Iowa, Kansas, Mandan, Missouri, Wichita, Omaha, Osage, Oto, Pawnee, Ponco, and Sioux—remained seminomadic, although their dependence on the buffalo increased when they acquired horses.

As buffalo-hunting intensified, the Indians became increasingly dependent on the animals for their essential needs: food, clothing, tools, bedding, weapons, and shelter. Even dried dung chips were burned for fuel.

Rituals and ceremonies preceded or followed every buffalo hunt. Blackfoot and Hidatsa medicine men, or *shamans*, hung a "buffalo rock," wrapped in a small calfskin pouch, from a tripod behind their tipi. The "rock," believed to have supernatural powers to control the herds, bore only a crude resemblance to a buffalo. The shaman paid tribute to the "buffalo rock" each morning and evening to attract herds into the region.

The Cheyenne attracted buffalo with shrill "calls," made by rubbing a carved elk antler against an antelope shin bone. The Mandans held elaborate Bull Dances, and the Pawnee played games believed to have magical powers. When a herd appeared, credit was given to the attending ceremony. If no herd appeared, the ceremony was repeated with stricter adherence to ritual.

Each hunt was carefully planned and executed by a Governing Council. Because it was a joint effort, every hunter became involved, and discipline was rigidly enforced. Any person acting on his own could scare away the herd and cause starvation.

Commonly used hunting techniques included: surrounding or encircling the herd; impounding it in a corral; driving

Impounding buffalo.

it over a cliff, onto ice, or up a canyon. The Cree, Assiniboin, Blackfoot, Gros Ventre, Cheyenne, and Crow were
masters at impounding. They built large, circular corrals,
300–400 feet in diameter, with vertical wood posts. A
twenty- or thirty-foot-wide corral entrance was approached
by a sloping, sod-covered ramp that rose to a height of eight
feet. When the animals fell off the end of the ramp into the
corral, they could not climb back out.

A shaman hung charms from a pole in the center of the
corral and placed ritual offerings on the ground. Then he
sent out four hunters to scout for buffalo. If the hunters had
to travel fifty miles in search of a herd, the shaman sometimes remained in the corral for several months. When a
herd was sighted, additional hunters coaxed the animals toward the corral site by mimicking buffalo and setting fires
under their hooves. When the shaman saw the herd, he
made a final offering to the medicine pole and left the cor-

ral. Men, women, and children then camouflaged themselves with sod, buffalo chips, sticks, and small tipi-like structures and formed a human, V-shaped fence, that extended from the entrance of the corral into the prairie. The wide end of the V was almost a mile across. Hunters stood close together along the ramp at the approach to the corral, where the buffalo might sense a trap and try to break away. Riders, covered with robes, leaned forward on their horses, creating a hump-back appearance, much like a buffalo, from a distance. The buffalo followed the riders.

The technique of encircling a herd worked most effectively on horseback. The riders circled loosely around the herd, then narrowed the circle before the animals became suspicious. If the wind was blowing, a gap was left in the circle in the direction of the wind and closed at the very last minute. Riders fired as many arrows as possible into the animals.

Cree Indians maneuvered buffalo onto icy lakes and rivers, a hunting technique they learned from wolves. In the northern Plains, where the Indians knew the rugged terrain better than the buffalo, they encircled and chased herds over steep cliffs.

Hunters on foot killed buffalo with long wooden lances, fitted with stone or bone blades. Later, when the Indians acquired horses, bows and arrows (fitted with flint or bone blades) were used. Riders carried large quantities of arrows because they fired them so rapidly.

In the north, many tribes hunted all winter. Herds became trapped in snow drifts, over which the Indians moved quite easily on snowshoes. This method of hunting was also done by women and children.

As a rule, activities surrounding the buffalo were communal, except for the processing of the meat. Hidatsa and Miami hunters gave the job of butchering to women because they felt it was mere drudgery. The Blackfoot, on the other

A Dakota woman preparing buffalo hides. (Smithsonian Institution)

hand, felt the job required strength and dexterity that women didn't have, so only the men were allowed to butcher.

Meat, organs, and some of the bones were wrapped in buffalo hides at the site of the kill and carted on horseback to camp. Hidden in the brush along the trail were wolves, foxes, coyotes, badgers, ravens, eagles, and vultures—all patiently waiting their turn to pick over what was left of the buffalo carcasses. If the site was close to an Indian encampment, packs of dogs joined the wild animals.

Large, unworked buffalo bone made excellent hammers and clubs, while roughly-split bone was fashioned into punches, awls, scrapers, and knives. Tribes of the Plains did not develop a weaving industry because women were too busy working buffalo hides. They made buffalo organs into waterproof containers and bags, or *parflèches*.

Special bone and antler tools were used to dress buffalo

41

*Hide scrapers and
skin dressers.* (Idaho
Historical Society)

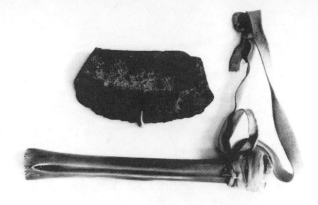

*Assiniboin necklace
made of animal
teeth and beads.
(Eastern Washington
State Historical Society.)*

*Paint shells with
bone paint brushes.
(Idaho Historical So-
ciety)*

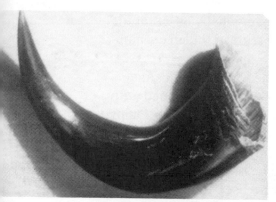

Buffalo horn. (East-
ern Washington
State Historical So-
ciety.)

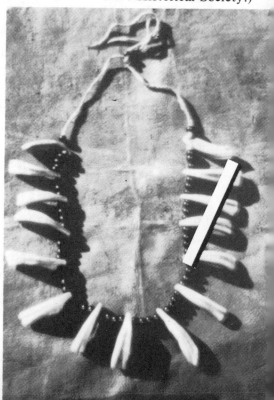

hides. A serrated buffalo leg bone was made into a chisel-like scraper to remove chunks of fat and flesh from the insides of the hides and fur off the outsides. A thick mixture of cooked buffalo brains, liver, and fat were spread on top of the hides and left to dry in the sun. Then the skin was washed in water. The following day, it was wrung out and left to bleach in the sun.

A large piece of buffalo bone, usually the femur or humerus, was split at one end to expose the sharp, spongy-looking interior. The bone was used to remove any remaining fibers left on the hide. Hides were soft-tanned by pulling them back and forth across a piece of taut sinew, tied between two trees. The pulling caused enough friction to both dry and soften the skins.

Hides were often painted with beautiful designs. The spongy end of a femur or humerus bone was used as a paint-brush because it was porous enough to hold the paint and allow the artist to create a smooth design. Separate bone brushes were used for each paint color.

Tribes of the Blackfoot made bowls and spoons of buffalo and sheep horns. Horns were placed in the fire until the gluey inside material could be easily removed. When the horn was cool enough to handle, it was rough-cut to the desired shape with a sharp bone knife. Then, it was softened in boiling water and placed over a rounded rock. A handle was bent into shape and held with stone weights. When the horn was dry, it became hard and retained its molded shape. The bowl or spoon was then smoothed with sandstone and polished with a piece of hide.

Blackfoot tribes made necklaces out of fish vertebrae, berries, roots, bear and eagle claws, and buffalo and elk teeth. By 1770, European traders had introduced glass and china beads, and Indian artists made them into necklaces. Eventually, beads of glass and china replaced natural materials in jewelry and clothing decorations.

6

SOUTHEAST

Tribes of the Southeast were primarily farmers, although fishing, shellfish-gathering, and hunting were also important seasonal activities. There was much serviceable stone and hardwood for toolmaking in the region, but shell, bone and antler were used as well. The soft, fine-grained bald cypress of the area was carved into utensils, masks, and figurines with shell and bone knives. Wooden canoes and mortars were hollowed out by burning the wood, then scraping it with clam shells.

In shallow coastal waters, fish were trapped in weirs woven of reeds and splints. The traps were designed to allow the fish to swim into them but could not get out. Southeastern tribes used nets, spears, and trot lines. A trot line, stretched across the length of a stream, had several shorter lines dangling in the water. Attached to each was a U-shaped turtle bone fishhook. Fishermen pulled themselves along the trot line in a dugout canoe to rebait or to remove the fish from the shorter lines.

The many rivers, lakes, and coastal estuaries in the Southeast once abounded with big fish—some of the largest in North America. Cane shafts, fitted with the tails of horseshoe crabs or stingrays, were used to spear the fish.

Inland tribes dug quantities of large, freshwater mussels from the muddy waters of the Mississippi and its tributaries. Freshwater mussels often grew up to six inches long. The shells were made into scoops, dishes, and cups. Often, the umbo, or hinge region of the shell, was carved into a handle. The inner linings of the mussels—pearly and quite beautiful—were used to make buttons in Colonial America.

In the fall, deer were hunted when they fed on acorns. Groups of hunters lit a circular fire around a herd, forcing them into a small area. Individual hunters also used deer decoys, made from a hollowed deer's head. The antlers were hollowed out to make them lightweight, and a portion of the hide was left attached. The disguise was easy to carry and simple to put on in a hurry.

Bears were hunted in tall hollow trees in winter. Because the animals were scarce, their claws, teeth, fur, and bones

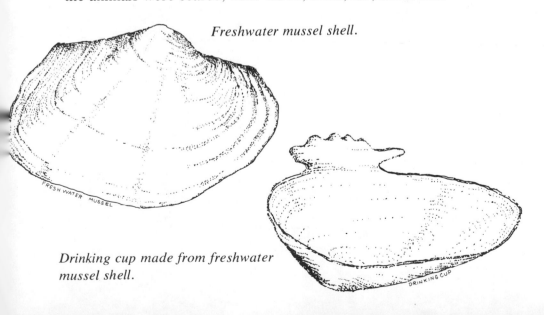

Freshwater mussel shell.

Drinking cup made from freshwater mussel shell.

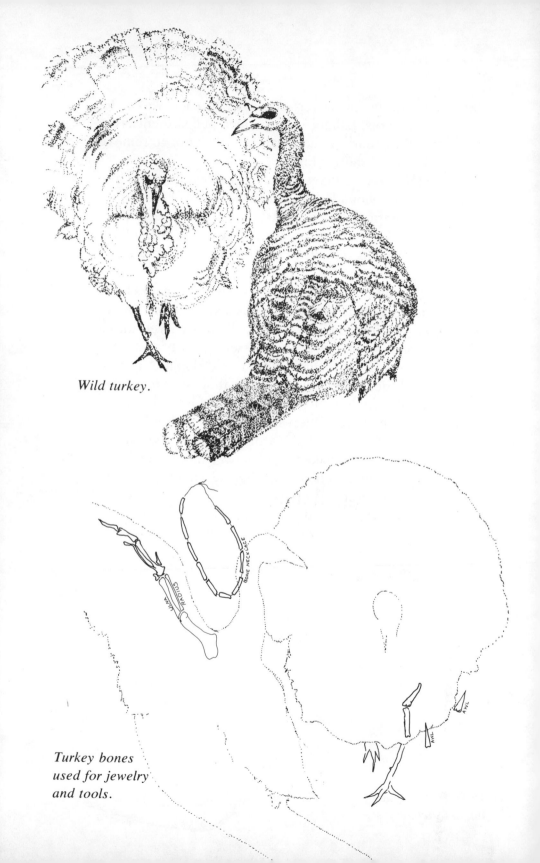

Wild turkey.

*Turkey bones
used for jewelry
and tools.*

were valuable raw materials. Beer teeth, spaced between beads, were made into bracelets and necklaces.

Waterfowl were plentiful in mid-October and in mid-April along the Mississippi flyway. Wild turkeys and passenger pigeons were important year-round food sources that also yielded bone material for fishhooks, awls, and needles. Turkey and turtle bones were popular materials for ornaments and hairpins. Tribes of the Cherokee used bone, antler, animal teeth, stone, and copper from the Southern Appalachians to make collars, bracelets, and earrings. They continued to work with traditional materials into the nineteenth century.

Tribes of Florida enjoyed miles of warm-water coast along the Atlantic and Gulf of Mexico. The North Equatorial Current, or Gulf Stream, a river of warm water which circles clockwise in the Atlantic between North America and Europe, passes near the Florida Keys—a natural habi-

A Seminole skinning a wild turkey. (Smithsonian Institution)

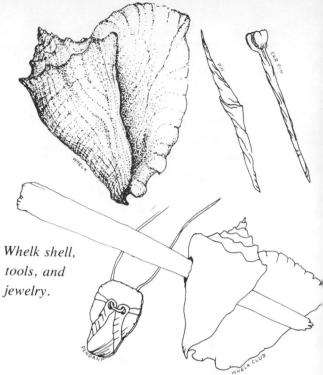

Contemporary elk horn pin, carved and painted by L. Riddle of the Osage tribe. (U.S. Department of the Interior, Indian Arts and Crafts Board)

Whelk shell, tools, and jewelry.

tat for shellfish. Some of the largest and most beautiful of the region are the whelk and conch. Tribes of the Southeast ate quantities of both species and collected the hard shells for making tools and ornaments, as well as for trade. Whelks and conchs are univalves with a central spiral that coils either to the left or to the right as the animals grow. The coiled portion, or *columellae,* was used for beads and pins, while the large, rounded section of the shells were made into bowls and scoops. Quantities of conch shell beads have been found as far inland as Oklahoma. Relatively light and unbreakable, they had great value as trade items. Tribes of the Great Lakes traded quantities of animal furs for the large shells. Gorgets, large round pendants worn about the neck, were made from the inner surfaces of the shells and were engraved with dancing scenes, animal figures, and geometric motifs. The designs were sometimes rubbed with black pigment to make them stand out. More elaborate gorgets had a combination of incising and cutout.

48

7

NORTHEAST

Tribes of the Northeast used tools made of stone, bone, shell, and antler to work the hardwood forests of the North. Fine-grained stone for toolmaking was plentiful in the region, and tribes were proficient at chipping and flaking the stone into high-quality tools. The strength and resiliency of antler made it the most desirable material for stone-flaking.

Northeastern tribes planted gardens of corn, beans, and squash. They created comfortable homes, sturdy canoes, and a variety of wooden utensils out of readily available wood. Although wood was most often worked with stone axes, gouges, and chisels, coastal tribes also used shell. Beaver incisors were preferred by many craftsmen to carve bowls, spoons, and for a variety of other utensils and ornaments.

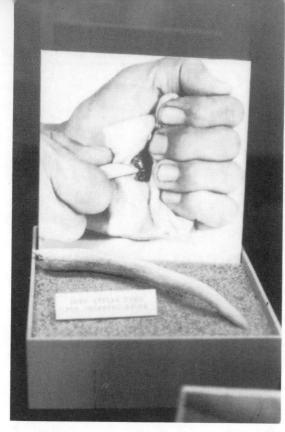

Antler flaking tool.

North of the Abenaki in Maine and Northeastern Canada, the summer growing season was very short, and tribes of the region had to hunt all winter. Caribou, moose, and elks were plentiful in the surrounding forests. Moose, traveling alone rather than in herds, were expertly tracked by hunters wearing wooden snowshoes.

Many northern tribes lived inland from the coast in bark-covered wigwams and tipis during the winter. In the summer, they removed the bark from their winter homes and carried it to the coast to cover their summer dwellings. In the spring, spawning Atlantic salmon were speared with twelve-foot, bone-headed harpoons. Among Maine tribes, bone fish hooks were also used to catch small freshwater fish. Bone and antler spears and arrowheads were used to hunt seals, walrus, and a variety of birds that nested along the rocky coast. Common clams were gathered as far north as Greenland, and oysters were found as far north as Cape Breten Island. Both quahogs and oysters thrived in a unique pocket of warm water in the Bay of Chaleur near Prince Edward Island. Indians of this region collected quantities of both species and used antler wedges to pry open the shells.

A flat, narrow coastal plain, south of New Hampshire, is crisscrossed with freshwater rivers and streams that once teemed with sturgeons, shads, eels, suckers, chain pickerels, and walleyed pikes. Fish and shellfish were abundant along the coast, and deer, black bears, racoons, opossums, rabbits, squirrels, foxes, and wolves were common in the nearby mountains. Tribes planted small gardens inland in the spring and spent the summer on the coast. Large pine logs were made into sturdy canoes by burning and scraping out the centers with shell and bone scrapers. Possessions were packed into the canoes and transported back and forth to the coast each season.

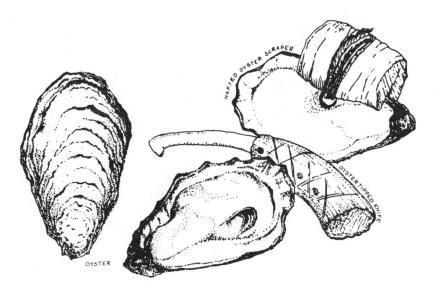

Oyster shells and tools.

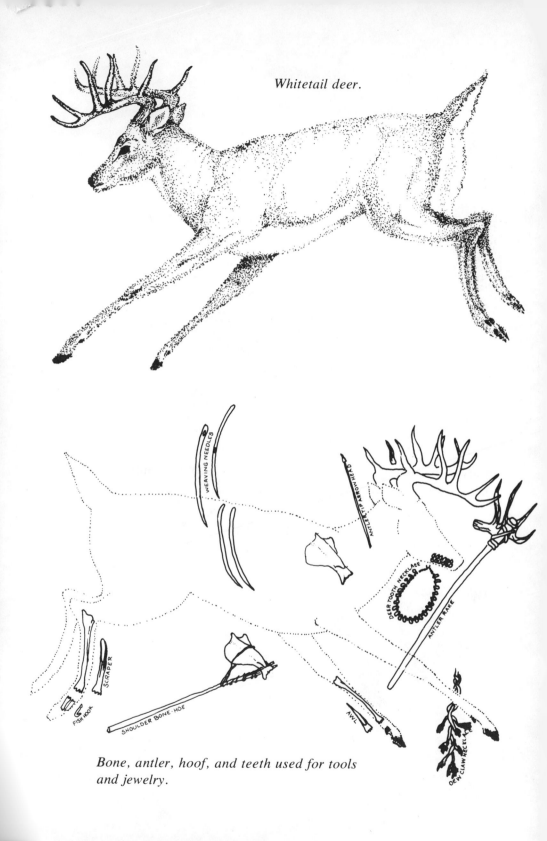

Whitetail deer.

Bone, antler, hoof, and teeth used for tools and jewelry.

White-tailed deer supplied tribes of the region with quantities of meats, furs, bones, and antlers. Deer feed along the edge of forests so they can dart into the trees to hide. In the summer, they are attracted to grassy areas near fresh water. Winter is the most difficult time for deer because the deep snow prevents them from traveling far enough to obtain sufficient food. During periods of very deep snow, they congregate among pine trees and help each other pack trails out into the woods in search of browse. Deer begin to grow antlers in the spring that become hard by the fall. The moderately spreading antlers are shed in December and January. The tines of the antlers are pointed and rise sharply from the burr, or beam, of the main shaft. Antlers were made into arrowheads, knives, and scrapers for dressing hides. Deerhide moccasins and robes were sewed with sinew, threaded through a fine-eyed bone needle.

South of Cape Cod, along the coasts of Rhode Island, Connecticut, and New York, shell-fishing was an important seasonal activity. Tribes weeded large gardens with clam-shell hoes, and clam and mussel shells were so plentiful that they were used for bowls, spoons, and scoops. Smooth shell fragments were used to scrape and polish pottery.

Hide fleshers were made from moose leg, probably the cannon bone of the animal. One end of the bone was cut away, then sharpened and serrated. Turkey-bone fish hooks were used to catch small fish, and the fish were scaled with shell knives and scrapers.

Large, freshwater mussels were once abundant along rivers, ponds, lakes, and streams. The shells were used for dishes and spoons. Very large mussel shells, for scraping and digging, were perforated near the hinge and hafted (a handle added). Shell knives, set in antler handles, were used to carve wooden bowls and spoons. Conch shells, traded with inland tribes in prehistoric times, were later used as ballast in ships coming from the Caribbean.

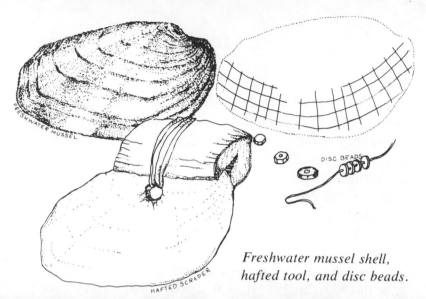

Freshwater mussel shell, hafted tool, and disc beads.

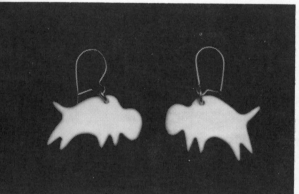

Beef bone earrings carved in shapes of buffaloes. (U.S. Department of the Interior, Indian Arts and Crafts Board)

Carved beef bone pendant in the form of a girl. (U.S. Department of the Interior, Indian Arts and Crafts Board)

Tribes of the Great Lakes harvested wild rice and hunted racoons, rabbits, squirrels, and deer in the hardwood forests of the region. Grassy prairie land, south of the Great Lakes, encouraged bears and herds of deer, elk, and buffalo to frequent the area. Birch and hickory bark were the most easily worked materials of the region. The Chippewa gathered the bark to build their wigwams and lightweight bark canoes. They also twined fine, tight baskets and mats out of cattails, rush, nettles and basswood bark. The basswood bark was made smooth and straight for weaving by shredding it through the pelvic bone of a small animal.

Turkey and rabbit-bone awls were used for weaving. Long, curved, deer and elk rib, perforated in the center or at one end, were made into needles for sewing.

Bones, shells, and antlers were made into a variety of ornaments. Necklaces were made of turkey, deer, and rabbit bones, combined with trade beads. Sashes were often decorated with toe bones and bear teeth.

Dewclaws were used for necklaces by tribes of the Great Lakes. The dewclaw is located above the true hoof in deer. It is similar to the functionless digit on the inner side of a dog's leg. The dew claws were soaked in hot water, trimmed to the desired shape, and often decorated with notches, serrations, and holes.

The rough interior ends of the deer's femur and humerus bones, where marrow is the thickest, were used to make painted pendants that were notched, grooved, and perforated.

Deer teeth were painted a reddish-purple hue, then strung on cords. Bearclaw fetishes, or charms, were worn by shamans to ward off evil spirits. The medicine tube was made of a section of a large animal bone, usually the femur or humerus of elk or deer.

Shell ornaments of disc and tubular beads were made from freshwater mussels. Circular and triangular shell pendants were also carved from the pearly centers of the mussels. Along the coast, quahog shells were cut into large disc pendants, then polished and engraved with designs of circles, stars, and half-moons.

Tribes of the Northeast were probably best known for their shell money, or *wampum*. The Algonkian word for a string of cylindrical beads was called *wampampeag*, which the Dutch shortened to wampum. Prior to the arrival of European settlers, Native Americans created cylindrical beads out of wood, and only rarely included cylindrical shell beads. After the introduction of iron, nails were set into the handles of grinding tools.

Most of the white wampum was made from the columella of whelks and conchs. We rarely use the large, older quahog shells because clams of this size were too old and tough to eat. But older quahogs often have a thick, purple edge. These edges were cut into small pieces and drilled. Each piece was drilled from the ends toward the center. About twenty rough-cut beads were strung on a cord, held tightly between both hands, and rolled back and forth across a grooved grindstone until the edges became round. The value of wampum is well-appreciated by anyone who has ever tried to cut or drill a hole in quahog shells; even power tools heat up and break.

Spherical, oval, and disc-shaped beads were produced by Native Americans long before the arrival of Europeans. Shells were cut and ground with abradors of stone and sand. Water was poured over the shells to prevent them from heating and cracking.

Colonial America was short of silver and gold currency, but could obtain quantities of furs from the Indians in exchange for shell beads. As a result, colonists set up bead production at various spots along the Hudson River and manufactured the bulk of wampum from 1650 to 1800. Five purple beads were worth a penny; purple beads were worth

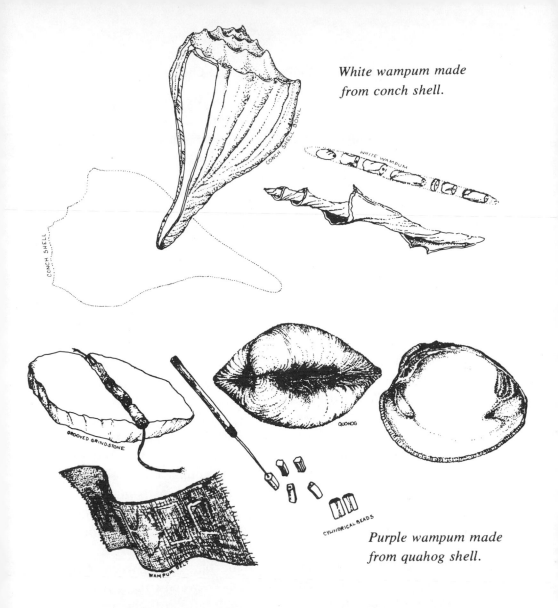

White wampum made from conch shell.

CONCH SHELL

CONCH SHELL BOWL

WHITE WAMPUM

GROOVED GRINDSTONE

QUOHOG

CYLINDRICAL BEADS

WAMPUM BELT

Purple wampum made from quahog shell.

Hiawatha wampum belt. (New York State Museum)

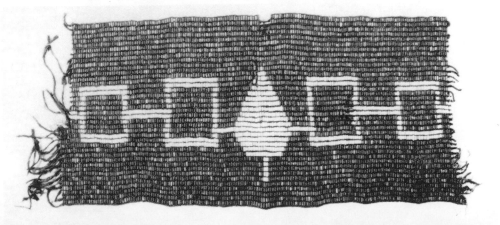

two or three times more than white wampum, often made of clamshells. By the eighteenth century, the value of purple and white wampum was about the same. Europeans continued to favor silver and gold, but the Indians preferred shell money.

Indian men plucked their hair and decorated their heads with shells. Women wore strings of wampum around their hair and strung wampum beads on tongs for bracelets, necklaces, and earrings. As in other areas of North America, it was common practice to bury the dead with all of their shell ornaments.

Most of the wampum we see today in museums is in the form of woven belts that carry messages or record historic events. Special designs were woven with purple and white wampum for these occasions. Hiawatha, believed to be one of the founders of the Iroquois League, or Five Nations, had a belt designed to represent the tribes of the powerful League: Mohawk, Oneida, Onondaga, Cayuga and Seneca.

One person was placed in charge of wampum belts, and each year he read the stories on them to other members of the tribe to refresh their memories. Young boys were encouraged to join their fathers when a belt was being read.

The Onondaga kept the wampum belts for the Five Nations. In the Michigan region, the Wyandot were the belt keepers. Occasionally, belts were painted. Red was the most popular color, then green and blue. Belts were also used as a means of communication between tribes. If one tribe sent a belt to another as a declaration of war, the receivers sent a reply in the form of a similar belt. Red paint on a belt with a hatchet design represented war. Peace treaties were ratified with other kinds of wampum belts. Some tribes also presented strings or belts of wampum to other tribes and to European settlers as gestures of friendship. Because the Europeans did not always understand the purpose of wampum-giving, they sometimes kept the belts.

8

HOW TO LOCATE SHELLS

Native Americans ate a variety of shellfish and used the discarded shells for tools and ornaments. Shellfish, still an important part of the American diet, are gathered along the Atlantic and Pacific coasts, the Gulf of Mexico, and in lakes, streams, rivers, and ponds. You can collect shellfish by digging for the particular species in your area.

Shellfish, or mollusks, wear their skeletons on the outside. This skeleton, or a shell, houses the animal's head, foot, and internal organs. When young, or in the larval stage, they are free-swimming. Unencumbered by a hard outer shell, young shellfish can travel many miles in water. The shell of the animal begins to grow in the larval stage, and within a short period, the shell restricts movement.

59

Like other animals, shellfish grow and reproduce where there is ample food and where environmental conditions are favorable. Some mollusks travel into shallow water during breeding season, while others never move except to feed or to escape prey.

Bivalves are mollusks with two separate shells, hinged together on one side. They are primarily sand or mud dwellers that move through layers of loose sand or mud while feeding on microscopic plant material. A special muscle closes the two shells and an elastic ligament holds the shell open during feeding. Oysters and jingles, two bivalves that do not move when feeding, attach themselves permanently to a piece of wood, a rock, or some other object.

Univalves are mollusks with only a single, spiral-like (coiled) shell. They feed on microscopic animals, and have an operculum on the back of the foot. The operculum is a horny plate that closes the shell when the animal wants to withdraw inside. Univalves, popular with North American Indians, include: abalone, conus, olive, olivella, cowrie, conch, and whelk.

The outer shell of mollusks, once used by Native Americans for tools and ornaments, is often very hard and strong. Glands along a fleshy mantle under the shell produce a lime-like material that makes the shell grow. Growth is periodic—sometimes occurring in a few days or weeks or during a season. The structure of shells is in the form of calcium carbonate. Crystals, deposited like bricks, are held together with a mollusk protein called conchiolin. The size and rate of shell growth is often determined by water temperature. Warm water encourages growth, and large conch and whelk shells are found in the warm waters of the Caribbean, the Gulf of Mexico, and along the coasts of Florida.

Most shells reach maturity between one and six years. However, the very large conchs live from ten to twenty-five years. The Atlantic Bay scallop, whose average life is eleven months, sometimes survives as long as twenty-five years.

Shell colors are determined by the kind of pigment cells in an animal's mantle. Yellow and orange are the most common shades.

LIGHTNING WHELK (Busycon contrarium)

Whelks are univalves that develop very heavy shells with large spines on the shoulder. For the last four thousand years, whelk shells were very important to many Eastern tribes. At least six species may be found in shallow Atlantic waters, from New Jersey to Florida. Older whelks are usually white. Younger ones are characterized by brown streaks that circle the bodies of the shells. While some whelks coil clockwise, or dextrally, the Lightning whelk coils counterclockwise, or sinistrally.

Most whelks feed on hard-shelled clams. They use their muscular feet to grip the clams and pull open the valves enough to insert tubular feeding organs, called probosces, into the soft body of a clam. The body of one clam is enough food to satisfy a whelk for a month.

ATLANTIC DEEP-SEA SCALLOPS (Placopecten magellanicus)

Scallops are one of the few bivalves that swim. Rather than lying on the ocean floor, waiting for food to pass by, scallops move to where they can get food and escape predators.

The shell of the scallop evolved to accommodate the animal's need to swim. It is lightweight and deeply ridged for added strength. To swim, a strong muscle, the adductor, enables the animal to open and close its valves. This action creates water turbulence that propels the animal along. To keep the valve open when the muscle is relaxed, there is an elastic cushion in the hinge.

61

Atlantic deep-sea scallops can be collected off the coast of Long Island in water up to eighty feet deep. The round, grayish-pink shells are collected by commercial fishermen for the edible adductor muscles inside the valves.

NORTHERN GREEN ABALONE (Haliotis walallenis stearns)

Abalone are dish-shaped univalves that generally live in shallow water, where they cling tightly to the bottom of the sea and feed on algae. Eight species live in the Pacific Ocean, from California to Mexico. They are gathered by Native Americans for food, and the large shells were used for utensils and ornaments. The iridescence of the shells made them especially valuable, and the shells were traded throughout North America.

Abalone is still gathered by California fishermen who sell the meat to restaurants. Rock crabs, octopuses, sea otters, and other fish feed on abalone. An abalone can escape predators by clamping itself tightly to the bottom of the ocean or by scurring off on its one foot.

Northern Green abalone are still fairly common in California waters, and may be identified by their red-blue outer shells covered with fine lines. The interiors of the shell are silver-green. There are natural holes along the edges of the shells through which the animals pass water and waste. Northern Green abalone are characterized by thier flat, elongated shells.

9

HOW TO CLEAN SHELLS

Materials

Shells
Pot of water
Methyl or isopropyl alcohol (optional)
Grain or ethyl alcohol (optional)
Sharp knife

1. Live shellfish must be cleaned, otherwise the tiny
    animal inside will rot and emit an unpleasant
    smell. Most shells respond to a few simple
    methods of cleaning, Boil the shellfish for 5 min-
    utes, starting with lukewarm water. Increase the

63

water temperature slowly to prevent cracking the shells. When they have cooled enough to handle, scrape the inside with a sharp knife. The animal will come right out.

2. Another method is to soak the animals overnight in a solution of 50 percent methyl or isopropyl alcohol or 70 percent grain, or ethyl alcohol.

3. The easiest way of all to clean shellfish is to set the animals out of doors, far from the house, and let nature's creatures have a feast. The shells will be cleaned in just a few days.

4. If you cannot dig for live shellfish, collect shells that are washed ashore along the coast. You can also ask your local fishmarket for discarded shells that storekeepers are often willing to give away. Shells may also be purchased from shell dealers. A list of dealers is included in the back of the book.

10

HOW TO MAKE SHELL KNIVES

Materials

Clam or scallop shells
Mini-honing stone
Large honing stone
#2 medium half-round file
Dusk mask
Drill press with cone sander (optional)
Mallet

1. Very sharp knives can be made with shell frag-
    ments. Break a large shell into pieces with a blunt
    mallet. Don't hammer too hard because pieces

Left:
Sharpening shell
with a file.

Below:
This group is making
shell knives with
honing stones and
files.

may fly at your face or the shell may splinter into pieces too small for use.

2. The edge of a large shell can be sharpened on both sides with the flat side of a #2 medium half-round file or with the flat side of a honing stone. Put on a dust mask. Grasp the shell firmly in one hand, rest it on your lap, and sand both sides of the shell edge until it is very sharp.

3. A shell can be scalloped with the round side of the #2 medium half-round file, or it can be serrated with the edge of a small honing stone. It can also be filed flat with a large honing stone.

4. If you want to scallop a shell edge, hold the shell edge firmly against a cone-shaped sander attached to a drill press. Scallop at even intervals along the shell edge.

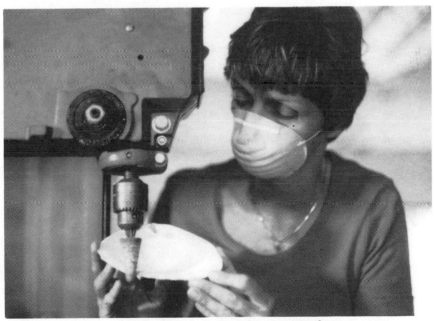

Scalloping a shell with power tools.

11

HOW TO MAKE SHELL CONTAINERS

Materials

Abalone or whelk shells
Pot of water
Commercial parafin and double boiler or pine
  pitch
Large spoon
#2 medium half-round file
Aluminum foil
Dremel Moto-Tool with #400 steel saw
Dust mask
Crayon

1. Abalone shells can be made into waterproof containers by filling in the natural holes along the side

68

HOW TO MAKE SHELL CONTAINERS

of the shell. Wrap the outside of the shell in several layers of aluminum foil to form a mold to hold the pitch when it is poured into the holes. (Collect pine pitch where it seeps from a tree wound. Old wounds, as well as new ones, yield globs of pitch.) Remove as much of the organic matter as possible from the pitch and boil it for 2 minutes. Scoop the pitch from the pot as it floats to the top and spoon it into the holes in the shell. If pine pitch is not obtainable, melt commercial parafin in a small double boiler. (PARAFIN IS HIGHLY FLAMMABLE AND MUST NOT BE MELTED OVER DIRECT HEAT.)

Collecting pine pitch.

Marking columellae of whelk.

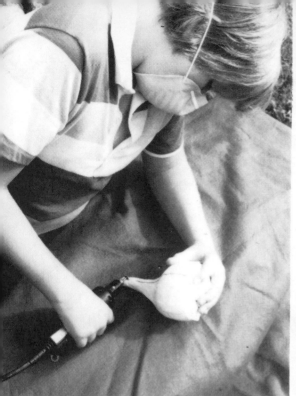

Cutting shell with a Dremel tool.

Abalone shell container and cut whelk shell container.

2. Whelk shells can be made into deep scoops or containers by cutting out the central spiral, or columellae. Make a line on the *outside* of the shell by gripping the central spiral on the inside with one hand while drawing a line with a soft dark crayon on the outside—as close to the central spiral as possible. Score the shell along the crayon mark with the tip of a #2 file so that the cutting blade will not slip on the smooth surface when you cut with the power tool. Put on a dust mask. Cut the shell in half with a Dremel Moto-Tool with a #400 circular steel saw. Allow the shell to cool every few minutes. Proceed slowly and don't press the saw too deeply into the shell as it cuts.

70

12

HOW TO MAKE A SHELL FISH HOOK

Materials

Shells (assorted)
Tree branch, approximately 3 feet long and 1 inch
 in diameter
Flat valve of Atlantic deep-sea scallop or piece of
 shell
Tree sealer
Punch
Pliers
#2 medium half-round file
Jeweler's saw with #2/0 cutting blade
Small table vise (optional)
Pump drill
Nylon fishing line, approximately 8 feet long
Dust mask

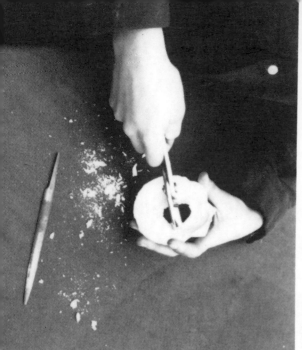

Breaking away a shell at its center.

Cutting away a hinge section.

Filing shell into a fish hook.

Tying a shell hook to a line.

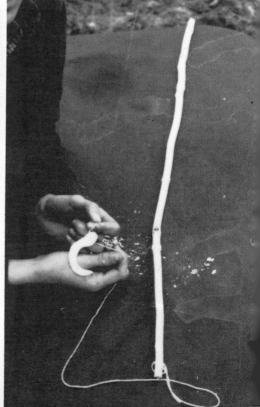

HOW TO MAKE A SHELL FISHHOOK

1. For a fishing pole, cut a 3-foot branch from a tree that needs pruning. Make the cut clean and close to the trunk. Paint the cut area with tree sealer to prevent the wood from becoming infected. Trim off all side branches, strip off the bark, and sand small knots to make a smooth handle.

2. Punch a hole in the center of a shell, using a hammer and punch. From the center, break away small pieces of the shell with a pair of pliers.

3. When the shell is reduced to approximately 3/4-inches around the circle, put on a dust mask and cut away the hinge section with a jeweler's saw.

4. File the lower end of the opening into a fine point, or fish hook design. File the other side smooth and drill a hole about 1/2 inch from the end.

5. Tie the fish line through the hole in the shell and attach it to the fishing pole.

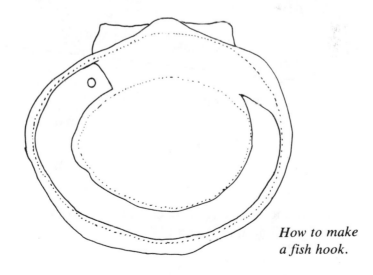

*How to make
a fish hook.*

13

HOW TO MAKE HAFTED SHELL TOOLS

Materials

Scallop shell
Clam shell
Hand saw
5-inch branch, approximately 1 inch in diameter
3-foot branch, approximately 3/4 inch in diameter
Tree sealer
Hammer
Punch
Coping saw
Rawhide or strong cordage, approximately 4 feet
#2 medium half-round file
Needle-nose pliers

HOW TO MAKE HAFTED SHELL TOOLS

1. Make a short-handled shell scraper with a scallop shell. Cut a 5-inch branch from a tree that needs pruning. Make the cut clean and close to the trunk. Paint the cut area with tree sealer to prevent the wood from becoming infected. Trim the ends of the branch, strip off the bark, and sand off small knots to make a smooth handle. Cut a V-section out of the wood with a coping saw. Be sure the V is wide enough to insert the scallop shell hinge. Make a hole in the shell, close to the hinge, with a hammer and punch, then enlarge it to about 1/2 inch in diameter. Insert the hinge of the scallop in the V-cut of the wood handle and lash the two together with rawhide or strong cordage. Place the cord through the hole in the shell and up around the handle several times. Tie securely.

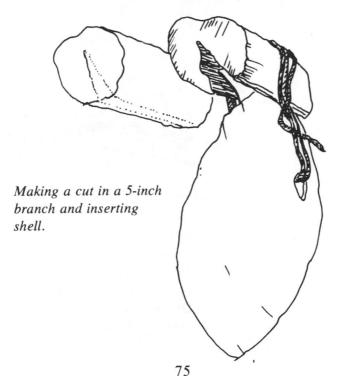

Making a cut in a 5-inch branch and inserting shell.

Tying a shell to a handle.

Attaching a long handle to a clam shell.

2. To make a long-handled shell shovel with a clam shell, cut a 3-foot branch from a tree in the same manner as above. Punch a hole in the clam shell near the hinge. Snip away some of the hinge with a pair of needle-nose pliers and place the branch on top of the hinge. Lash the shell and handle together, going through the hole in the shell and up around the handle with rawhide or cordage. Tie securely.

14

HOW TO MAKE A SHELL BRACELET

Materials

Scallop shell
#2 medium half-round file
Hammer
Punch
Pliers
Small round file
Dust mask

1. Punch or drill a hole in the center of the shell.

2. Enlarge the hole by snipping away small pieces

77

Carving a frog on the hinge of a shell bracelet.

Filing a shell into a circle.

from the center hole with pliers. Be careful not to break away pieces that are too large or you will fracture the shell edge.

3. Put on a dust mask. With the round side of the #2 medium half-round file, enlarge the center hole by filing gently in a circle until the edge is reduced to about 1/2 inch all around.

4. Carve a frog design on the umbo, or hinge, of the shell with a small round file or the end of the #2 file. To prevent the arch of the hinge from taking too much pressure while carving, place the bracelet on a folded towel.

78

15

HOW TO MAKE SHELL JEWELRY

Materials

Shell scraps (abalone, conch, scallop)
Conus, cowrie, snail shells
#2 medium half-round file
Jeweler's saw with #2/0 cutting blade
Small round file
Felt-tipped pen or china marker
Small table vise
Charcoal
Pump drill
Macrame cord
Small wooden or ceramic beads
Dust mask

A fish pendant cut from piece of abalone shell.

Incising a design on a conch shell.

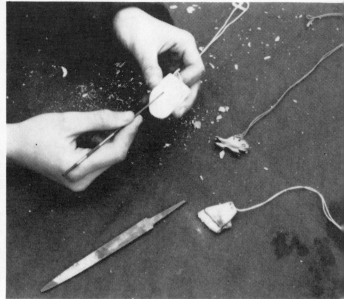

Inserting a cord through a hole in a conus shell.

Shells, beads, and bones, strung into bracelets and necklaces.

HOW TO MAKE SHELL JEWELRY

1. Pieces of shell can be made into interesting shapes for earrings, necklaces, pendants, and bracelets. Abalone is especially easy to cut with a jeweler's saw. Draw a design on a piece of abalone shell with a felt-tipped pen or china marker. *Remember to put on a dust mask before cutting the shell.* Clamp the shell piece into a table vise and cut out your design with the jeweler's saw. File the edges all around the design. Make a pendant by drilling a hole in the top of your piece and attaching it to a piece of macrame cord.

2. Break a shell into pieces and file one of the pieces into an interesting shape. Drill a hole in the top of the piece and attach it to a piece of macrame cord.

3. Conch shells have very shiny interiors that give satisfying results when incised. Draw a design on a piece of conch shell and incise it with the pointed end of the #2 medium half-round file. Fill in your design with charcoal. Grind the edges of the shell pieces until smooth. Drill a hole, or holes, in the top of the piece and attach it to a piece of macrame cord.

4. Enlarge the tiny hole in the top of conus or snail shells with a small round file. Push the macrame cord through the hole, aiming it at a small opening in the chamber along the outside wall. Alternate shells with beads to make a necklace, bracelet, or earrings.

16

HOW TO LOCATE BONES

The skeletons of most large mammals are basically alike. Individual bones have evolved in special ways to accommodate environmental adaptations made by the animal. Native Americans used bones from a variety of animals to create the same kinds of tools.

The long, slender, lower leg bone, or cannon bones, of deer, elks, moose, and caribou were used for tools that required great strength. These bones are particularly strong because these even-toed animals carry the main axis of their weight on their lower leg bones. The ulna bone of mammals has a natural finger grip that is well-suited for awls. Ulna bones were also used for weaving.

Buffalo ulna bones were strong and well-suited for

punching holes in leather. The bones of the animal differ from the bones of even-toed animals because buffaloes are short-legged and thick-bodied. The bones of domestic steer are so much like buffalo bones, that they are often confused. In fact, buffalo and steers were once grouped together in animal classification because they share a similar chromosomal structure and blood type. Buffaloes have a larger skull than steer and fourteen pairs of ribs; steer have only thirteen pairs of ribs. Buffaloes have been crossed with yaks and domestic humped cattle, but a line of hybrids has not been established because the male offspring of the hybrid strain has always remained sterile.

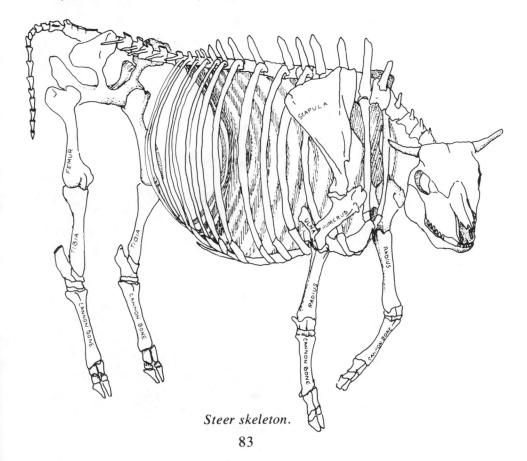

Steer skeleton.

Steer bones can be obtained from butcher shops and supermarkets. Beef cuts in supermarkets contain only cut-up
bones. Whole steer bones are extremely large, and a special
request for whole bones must be made to a butcher.

Many regions of North America have annual hunting seasons. United States Fish and Wildlife Agencies and state
fish and wildlife agencies monitor herds and allow hunting
when the number of animals exceeds the potential food
sources of the region. Hunters often take their animals to
butchers who specialize in dressing wild animals. Because
these butchers usually throw away excess bones, antlers,

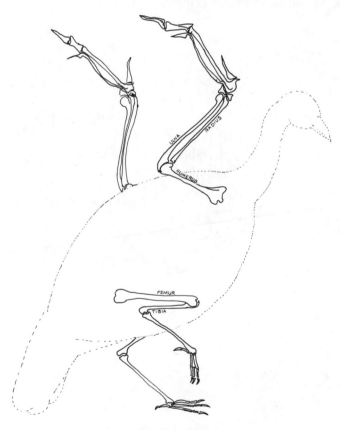

Turkey skeleton.

84

and hoof materials, they are often willing to give away discards.

Wild animals hit by cars or taken illegally are kept by state fish and wildlife agencies and auctioned off each year for their pelts. Bones and related material can sometimes be acquired at these auctions.

Domestic chickens and turkeys belong to a group of fowl-like birds that include pheasants, grouse, quails, guinea hens, and wild turkeys. The wings of these birds were used by Native Americans for beads, and the leg bones were made into strong awls, knives, and needles. Chicken and turkey bones are readily available from butcher shops, supermarkets, restaurants, and the family dinner table.

Bone-related materials, such as nails, claws, antlers, hooves, scales, feathers, hair, and teeth enamel grow from specialized skin cells that develop to suit the evolutionary needs of the animal. Tribes of North America used many of these materials for tools and ornaments. Some, still available, are fun to locate and work.

Deer and elk antler are solid, bony appendages that grow from the skull of the animal. Antlers—shed each year—can be obtained in the forests of North America, from wildlife refuges, and from hunters. In Jackson, Wyoming, the antlers of eight thousand elks, shed annually on the Federal Elk Refuge, are collected by boy scouts and auctioned off each year.

The horns of goats, sheep, buffaloes, steers, and pronghorn antelopes have bony cores, covered with an outer sheath. When removed, it is hollow. Hollow horns are mostly unbranched and remain on the animal until it dies. The pronghorn antelope is the exception because it sheds the sheath each year and the bony core persists on the skull.

Native Americans used hollow horns to mold cups, bowls, scoops, and spoons. Domestic goat horns are good substitutes.

17

HOW TO CLEAN BONES

Materials

Bones
Coping saw
Kitchen scissors
Pot, approximately 12'' in diameter
Axion
Pipe cleaners
Knife
Cookie sheet
Small animal cage

1. Remove as much cartilaginous material as possible

from the bones and cut off one end of each bone to be made into a scraper or awl. Cut both ends of the bones to be used for jewelry. Steer bones must be cut with a coping saw; fowl bones with a pair of kitchen scissors. Bones are easiest to cut when moist and fresh. Remove the marrow from inside the bones with pipe cleaners. Rinse the bones several times and put them in a clean pot of water. Boil fowl and steer bones *separately*.

2. Bring steer bones to a boil in 1/2 cup of Axion, and simmer for 4 to 5 hours. (The Axion will make the bones white.)

*Steer bones–scapula, ribs, ulna, and radius–
cleaned and ready to work.*

87

3. Bring fowl bones to a boil in 2 tablespoons of Axion and simmer 1 hour. Keep the water just at the *simmering* point. Prolonged, rapid boiling will weaken the bones.

4. Rinse the bones in cold water, then scrape away any remaining cartilaginous material. Rinse them several times before placing them in a fresh pot of water.

5. Repeat the Axion-simmering process in steps 2 and 3. This will remove all the fat from the bones. Thoroughly rinse them once again. Put the bones on a cookie sheet to dry. Steer bones may take a week to dry at room temperature. Fowl bones will be dry after one or two nights at room temperature. Bones may be dried in less time in a very low oven. The bones will be very hard and almost white when thoroughly dry.

6. The bones may be cleaned naturally by placing them in a small animal cage set outdoors away from the house. The cage protects the bones from large animals. Although this process may take several months, it is the easiest way to clean the bones.

18

HOW TO MAKE A BONE SCRAPER

Materials

Steer rib
#1 coarse half-round file
1 sheet medium grit sandpaper

1. Prepare the rib bone by following step 4 on page 88. The rib marrow is not removed, and the first boiling is unnecessary.

2. There is a natural grip at one end of the rib where it attaches to the animal's backbone. Grip the rib

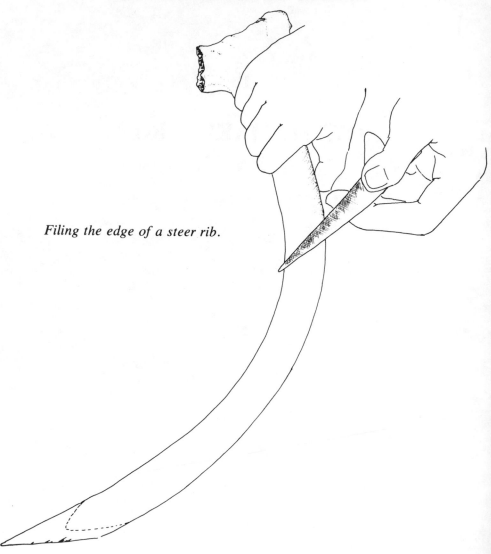

Filing the edge of a steer rib.

at this end and sharpen the bottom edge with the #1 coarse half-round file. Round the end of the scraper by filing off the sharp corners. File rough edges from the grip end, then sand the entire bone with medium grit sandpaper.

19

HOW TO MAKE A BONE AWL

Materials

Fowl bone legs (tibia)
Miscellaneous animal bones
Sharp rock (optional)
#2 medium half-round file
#1 coarse half-round file

1. The proximal end, or the end nearest the animal's heart, must be removed from chicken or turkey leg bones before the bones are boiled and cleaned. Prepare the bones according to the directions on page 86. Score a V the length of the fowl's leg

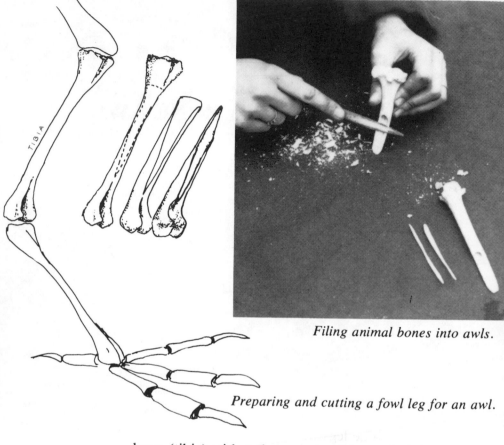

Filing animal bones into awls.

Preparing and cutting a fowl leg for an awl.

bone (tibia) with a sharp rock or the end of the #2 medium half-round file. File back and forth along the V until it snaps away from the bone. File the end of the bone to a point with the flat side of the file. File the V portion smooth along the edges.

2.   Prepare any strong piece of bone according to directions on page 86. File the end with the #1 coarse half-round file. (Because the leg bones of steers and deer are much stronger than fowl bones, a coarse awl is needed to file them.)

92

20

HOW TO MAKE A BONE FISH HOOK

Materials

       Lamb or deer toe bones
       Jeweler's saw with #2/0 cutting blade
       Small table vise
       Small round file
       Nylon fish line, approximately 12 feet long
       Pencil

1. Prepare the bones according to the directions on page 86. Only one boiling is necessary because toe bones are not cut until they are used. Place the toe bone in the vise and cut it in half lengthwise. A small amount of marrow will have to be washed

93

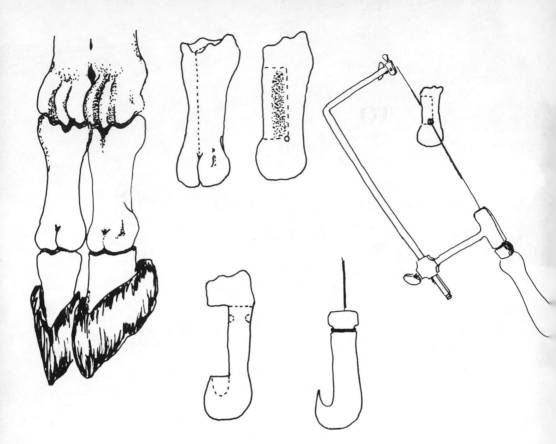

Where to cut toe bone.

away from the hollow interior of the bone. Each half can be made into a fish hook.

2. With a pencil, mark the place where the bone is to be cut. There should be two small cuts near each end and a vertical cut connecting the two. Use the jeweler's saw to cut each of the horizontal ends. To make the vertical cut, drill a small hole in one of the corners by a horizontal cut. Release one end of the blade from the jeweler's saw and thread it through the hole. Firmly place the blade into the saw, and put the bone in the vise with the saw attached. Saw the length of the bone along the ver-

94

Cutting a toe bone in half.

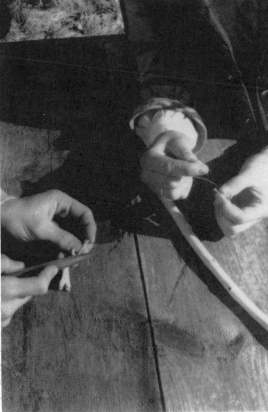

*The final preparation of
a hook, attaching the
hook to a nylon line.*

tical line until you reach the small horizontal cut at
the other end.

3. File the inside of the rounded end of the toe bone
   with the small round file until you have a hook
   shape.

4. Cut off the scalloped end of the bone, then file
   very tiny grooves along the straight side of the
   hook. Attach the nylon fish line and tie securely.
   (Don't cut off the scalloped end of the bone until
   the hook is shaped; you will need to grip onto it
   while filing.)

21

HOW TO MAKE A BONE HOE

Materials

Steer shoulder bone (scapular)
Wood saw
Sapling tree, approximately 5 feet long and 3
  inches in diameter
Hack saw
Screw driver, approximately 12 inches long
Hammer
Strong twine

1. Cut down a straight sapling tree, approximately 3
    inches in diameter, from an area that needs prun-

96

ing. Cut off side branches, trim off the top, and peel away the bark. It is important to use a freshly cut sapling for your hoe handle because the shoulder bone will be inserted in a slit at one end of the wood. Fresh wood is especially flexible.

2. Cut a notch in each side of the shoulder bone about 3'' from the broad end of the bone. Cut one V in the vertical protrusion along the back of the bone, even with the notches. (If the neck of the bone is wider than 3 inches, cut away a portion of bone from either side to fit your wood handle.)

3. Drive the screw driver into the very center of the thick end of the prepared handle. Hold the split open, and place the neck of the shoulder blade in the opening at a right angle to the handle. Gently hammer the shoulder bone into place.

Hammering a shoulder bone into the wedge of a handle.

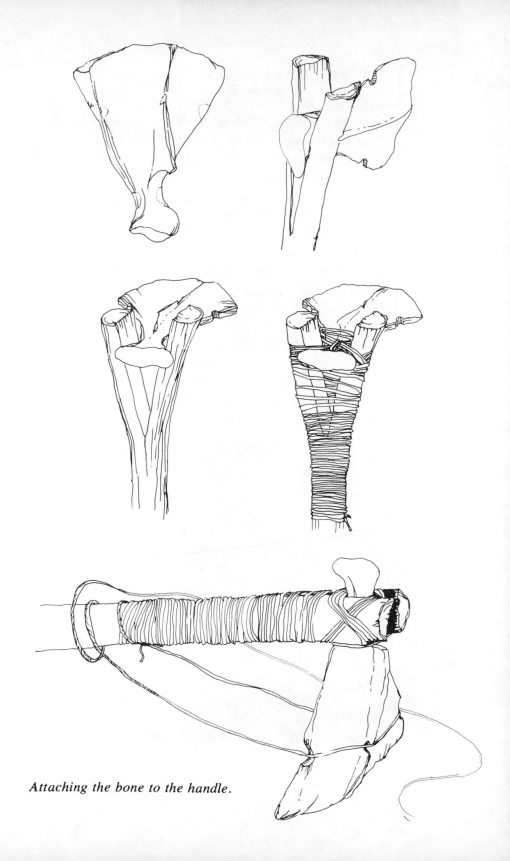

Attaching the bone to the handle.

Lashing the last piece of twine around the hoe handle.

4. About 12 inches below the handle, where the slit ends, tie on a 12 feet piece of strong twine, and wrap it around the handle up to the point where the bone is wedged between the wood. Continue to secure the handle to the bone by wrapping the twine in a criss-cross fashion around the end place where the bone is wedged into the slit in the handle. Tie off.

5. About 12 inches below the handle, tie another piece of twine, approximately 12 feet long, around the handle. Bring this piece of twine around the notch on one side of the broad end of the bone, through the notch in the vertical protrusion on the back of the bone, into the notch on the opposite side of the bone, and back to the handle. Loop the twine around the handle and repeat the wrapping process three more times.

22

HOW TO MAKE A BONE
BREASTPLATE

Materials

48 Radius bones from chicken wings
6 Ulna bones from chicken wings
72 Beads, approximately 5/16 inch in diameter
11 Beads, approximately 3/8 inch in diameter
6 Beads, approximately 1/4 inch in diameter
12 Pieces macramé cordage, approximately 10 inches long
1 Piece macramé cordage, approximately 17 inches long
1 Piece macramé cordage, approximately 24 inches long
2 Sheets of wet-and-dry sandpaper

100

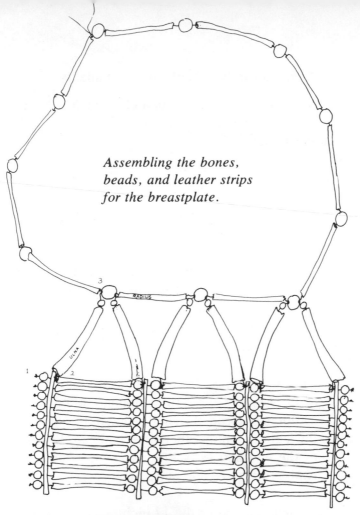

Assembling the bones, beads, and leather strips for the breastplate.

A student wears his finished breastplate.

4 Strips of leather, approximately 7 inches long
   and 1 inch wide
Leather punch
Red pen
Ruler

1. Prepare chicken wing bones according to directions on page 86.

2. Gently sand the bone ends by rubbing them against a flat sheet of wet and dry sandpaper.

3. Measure 12 holes, 3/8 inch apart, in each leather strip. Punch out the holes with a leather punch.

4. Line up the beads, leather strips, and bones in front of you. Take a 10-inch length of cordage, tie a knot in one end of it, and string it through a bead, the leather, a bone, then another bead. Repeat this to the end and tie a knot. Repeat again until all twelve rows are complete.

5. Attach one end of the 17-inch piece of cordage to the first section of the first row of the breastplate. Thread an ulna bone, a 1/4-inch bead, a 3/8-inch bead, a 1/4-inch bead, and an ulna bone. Attach them to the other end of the first section. Repeat this process twice.

6. Take the 24-inch piece of cordage and alternate a 3/8-inch bead with a radius bone five times. Push the cordage through the center of each V section, adding one radius bone between sections. Continue to add a radius bone and a 3/8-inch bead five times. Tie the ends together tightly.

23

HOW TO MAKE BONE JEWELRY

Materials

Cleaned chicken or turkey wing bones
Steer bones
#2 medium half-round file
Macramé cord, approximately 3 feet
2 Sheets, wet and dry sandpaper
Wooden or ceramic beads (approximately 2
   dozen)

1. Prepare the bones according to directions on page
    86. (If you want smaller beads, cut the bones into
    lengths *before* they are boiled.) Smooth the ends
    of the bones with a sheet of wet-and-dry sandpa-
    per. Sand the bones with another piece of the
    sandpaper.

2. Cut a length of macramé cord approximately 19 inches long for a necklace and a piece 10 inches long for a bracelet. Alternate bones and beads in a pleasing design. (Ulna bones are larger than radius bones and look better with larger beads.)

3. Rings can be made from steer bones by cutting off circles from a leg bone. Sand the outside edges smooth with the #2 medium half-round file and sand the surface of the ring with wet-and-dry sandpaper. Incise a design on the ring with the pointed end of the file, then fill in the design with charcoal.

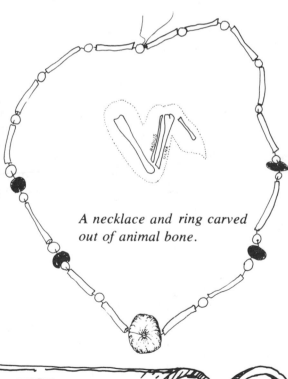

This student wears her necklace and bracelet of bones and beads.

A necklace and ring carved out of animal bone.

SHELL DEALERS

Shells of the Seas, Inc.
P.O. Box 1418
Ft. Lauderdale, Florida 33302

Tidepool Gallery of Minneapolis
3907 W. 50th Street
Edina, Minnesota 55424

Tidepool Gallery at Malibu
22762 Pacific Coast Highway
Malibu, California 90265

Seashells Unlimited, Inc.
590 Third Avenue
New York, New York 10016

Panamic Specimen Shells
3846 E. Highland
Phoenix, Arizona 95018

The Shell Shop
590 Embarcadero
Morro Bay, California 93442

The Shell Gallery
77 Union Street
Newton Centre, Mass. 02159

SELECTED BIBLIOGRAPHY

American Malacological Union, Inc. *How to Study and Collect Shells: A Symposium.* Wrightsville Beach, North Carolina, 1974.

Banfield, A. W. F. *The Mammals of Canada.* Toronto, Canada: University of Toronto Press, 1974.

Bergeron, Eugene. *How to Clean Seashells.* St. Petersburg, Florida: Great Outdoors Publishing Co., 1971.

Blessing, Fred, K. "Some Uses of Bone, Horn, Claws and Teeth by Minnesota Ojibwa Indians," *The Minnesota Archaeologist,* Vol. XX, No. 3, 1956. St. Paul, Minnesota.

Burt, Jesse, and Ferguson, Robert B. *Indians of the Southeast: Then and Now.* New York: Abington Press, 1973.

Chalfant, Stuart A. *Nez Percé Indians, Aboriginal Terri-*

tory of the Nez Percé Indians. New York: Garland Publishing, Inc., 1974.

Gunther, Erna. *Indian Life of the Northwest Coast of North America*. Chicago: University of Chicago Press, 1972.

Heizer, Robert F., ed. *Handbook of North American Indians*, Vol. 8, *California*. Washington, D.C.: Smithsonian Institution, 1978.

Horr, David Agee, ed. *Coast Salish and Western Washington Indians, II*. New York: Garland Publishing, Inc., 1974.
Paiute Indians, II. American Indian Ethnohistory, California, and Basin-Plateau Indians. New York: Garland Publishing, 1976.

Hudson, Charles M. *The Southeastern Indians*. Knoxville, Tennessee: University of Tennessee Press, 1976.

Jernigan, E. Wesley. *Jewelry of the Prehistoric Southwest*. Albuquerque: University of New Mexico Press, 1978.

Leftwich, Rodney L. *Arts and Crafts of the Cherokee*. Cullowhee, North Carolina: Land-of-the-Sky Press, 1970.

McHugh, Tom. *The Time of the Buffalo*. Lincoln, Nebraska: University of Nebraska Press, 1972.

Miles, Charles. *Indian and Eskimo Artifacts of North America*. New York: Bonanza Books, 1963.

Orchard, William C. *Beads and Beadwork of the American Indians*. New York: Museum of the American Indian, 1975.

Stewart, Hilary. *Indian Art of the Northwest Coast*. Seattle, Washington: University of Washington Press, 1975.

Trigger, Bruce G., ed. *Handbook of North American Indians*, Vol. 15, *Northeast*. Washington, D.C.: Smithsonian Institution, 1978.

COMMON METRIC EQUIVALENTS AND CONVERSIONS

Approximate

1 inch	= 25 millimeters
1 foot	= 0.3 meter
1 yard	= 0.9 meter
1 square inch	= 6.5 square centimeters
1 square foot	= 0.09 square meter
1 square yard	= 0.8 square meter
1 millimeter	= 0.04 inch
1 meter	= 3.3 feet
1 meter	= 1.1 yards
1 square centimeter	= 0.16 square inch

Accurate to Parts Per Million

inches × 25.4°	= millimeters
feet × 0.3048°	= meters
yards × 0.9144°	= meters
square inches × 6.4516°	= square centimeters
square feet × 0.092903	= square meters
square yards × 0.836127	= square meters

INDEX